5 Ingredients

Dash Diet

Cookbook for Beginners

150 Healthy and Low-Sodium Recipes with 21-Day Meal Plan to Lower Blood Pressure and Improve Your Health

Chris Lane

MW00334351

11.621

The content contained within this book may not be reproduced, duplicated, or transmitted without direct written permission from the author or the publisher. Under no circumstances will any blame or legal responsibility be held against the publisher, or author, for any damages, reparation, or monetary loss due to the information contained within this book, either directly or indirectly.

Legal Notice: This book is copyright protected. It is only for personal use. You cannot amend, distribute, sell, use, quote or paraphrase any part, or the content within this book, without the consent of the author or publisher.

Disclaimer Notice:

Please note the information contained within this document is for educational and entertainment purposes only. All effort has been executed to present accurate, up to date, reliable, complete information. No warranties of any kind are declared or implied. Readers acknowledge that the author is not engaged in the rendering of legal, financial, medical, or professional advice. The content within this book has been derived from various sources. Please consult a licensed professional before attempting any techniques outlined in this book. By reading this document, the reader agrees that under no circumstances is the author responsible for any losses, direct or indirect, that are incurred as a result of the use of the information contained within this document, including, but not limited to, errors, omissions, or inaccuracies

What is the DASH Diet?...8

The Benefits of the DASH Diet...9

What to Eat and What to Minimize on Dash Diet...10

Tips for Keeping the Dash Diet...11

Breakfast recipes...13

Chives and sesame omelet..13

Omelet with peppers...14

Cheese hash browns...14

Egg toasts...15

Curry tofu scramble...15

Walnut pudding...16

Fruits and rice pudding..16

Vanilla toasts...17

Blueberries mix...17

Sweet yogurt with figs...18

Strawberry sandwich...18

Almond crepes..19

Bean frittata..19

Bean casserole..20

Grape yogurt..20

Cherry rice..21

Whole grain pancakes..21

Breakfast almond smoothie..22

Baked fruits...22

Chia oatmeal..23

Millet cream...23

Tomato egg whites..24

Dill omelet..24

Side dishes..25

Tomato brussel sprouts...25

Milky mash..25

Basil corn..26

Fried zucchini...26

Sage asparagus..27

Quinoa bowl...27

Low-fat sour cream potato...28

Asparagus in sauce..29

Sweet paprika carrot...30

Cauliflower bake..30

Roasted carrot halves..31

Beans in blended spinach..31

Turmeric endives..32

Light corn stew...32

Aromatic cauliflower florets...33

Grilled tomatoes..33

Thyme potatoes..34

Dijon potatoes..34

Sesame seeds brussel sprouts...35

Braised baby carrot..35

Baked herbed carrot..36

Fragrant tomatoes..36

Parsley broccoli...37

Grinded corn...37

Grilled pineapple rings..38

Salads...39

Vegan salad..39

Tender green beans salad...39

Fish salad...40

Salad skewers..40

Fennel bulb salad..41

Watercress salad...41

Orange mango salad...42

Pine nuts salad..42

Shredded beef salad..43

Seafood salad with grapes..43

Tender endives salad...44

Smoked salad...44

Corn salad with spinach..45

Spring salad...45

Tropical salad...46

Bean sprouts salad...46

Tuna salad...47

Cucumber and lettuce salad..48

Vegan and vegetarian main dish..49

Cauliflower steaks...49

Honey sweet potato bake...49

Baked tempeh...50

Quinoa burger...50

Carrot cakes..51

Loaded potato skins...51

Spinach casserole...52

Tempeh reuben...52

Turmeric cauliflower florets..53

Beef and pork...54

Oregano pork tenderloin..54

Hoisin pork...54

White cabbage rolls..55

Fennel pork chops..55

Hot beef strips..56

Spiced beef...56

Spinach pork cubes..57

Fajita pork strips..57

Herbs de provence pork chops...58

Tender pork medallions..58

Baked beef tenders...59

Poultry..60

Chicken with red onion..60

Clove chicken...61

Chicken tomato mix...61

Turkey with olives..62

Soft sage turkey..62

5-spices chicken wings..63

Thai style chicken cubes..63

Pumpkin chicken..64

Asparagus chicken mix..64

Apple chicken...65

Lean chicken thighs..65

Glazed chicken..67

Spiced turkey fillet..67

Fish and seafood..**68**

Dill steamed salmon...68

Grilled tilapia...68

Mint cod...69

Clams stew..69

Limes and shrimps skewers..70

Juicy scallops...70

Salmon and corn salad..71

Spicy ginger seabass...71

Shallot tuna...72

Tomato halibut fillets..72

Salmon with basil and garlic...73

Salmon in capers...73

Yogurt shrimps...74

Turmeric pate...74

Tuna and pineapple kebob..75

Rosemary salmon..75

Herbed sole...76

Aromatic salmon with fennel seeds...76

Spiced scallops...77

Allspice shrimps..77

Desserts..**78**

Melon salad...78

Grilled peaches...78

Milk fudge..79

Rhubarb with aromatic mint..79

Mousse with coconut..80

Cardamom black rice pudding..80

Stuffed fruits...81

Lime cream...81

Lemon pie..82

Nigella mix...82

Poached pears..83

Baked apples...84

Fragrant apple halves...85

Chia and pineapple bowl...85

Fruit kebabs...86

Citrus pudding..86

Raspberry stew..87

Vanilla cream...87

Ginger cream..88

Mango rice...88

Apricot cream...89

Peach stew...89

Oatmeal cookies...90

21 days 5 Ingredients meal plan..91

What is the DASH Diet?

The main aim of the DASH diet is not to lose weight but to reduce blood pressure. However, it can also help those who want to lose weight, lower cholesterol, and manage or prevent diabetes.

Important aspects include:

- portion size

- consuming a wide variety of healthful foods

- obtaining the proper balance of nutrients

DASH encourages a person to:

- eat less sodium (the key ingredient in salt)

- increase their intake of magnesium, calcium, and potassium

- These strategies help lower blood pressure.

DASH is not a vegetarian diet, but it adds more fruits and vegetables, low or nonfat dairy foods, beans, nuts, and other nutritious items. It also provides suggestions about healthful alternatives to "junk food" and encourages people to avoid processed foods.

An expert panel has ranked DASH in the top two overall diets for several years in a row. U.S. News & World Report publishes their review of "best diets" every year, and DASH has been consistently in the number one or two position for almost a decade. Why? It's a sensible, healthy eating plan that's easy for most people to follow. Since it's not overly restrictive, people can stick with it.

Adopting an eating plan based on DASH doesn't just help people lower their blood pressure. Some of the other major benefits include the following:

1. Prevent Heart Disease and Strokes

Heart disease and stroke are two of the leading causes of death in the United States. Since high blood pressure is a primary risk factor, modifying your diet and lifestyle can help control this risk. It's worth noting that high blood pressure is also a risk factor for kidney disease, so DASH will reduce your risk for that condition, as well.

While follow-up research about DASH showed it can help lower blood cholesterol and reduce weight (both heart-disease risk factors), other studies showed a positive correlation between the diet and reduced heart-disease risk. The OmniHeart study (Optimal Macronutrient Intake Trial for Heart Health) compared three DASH-inspired diets with different carbohydrate, protein source, and fat parameters. One diet was rich in carbohydrates, one rich in protein (half from plant sources), and one rich in monounsaturated fat. All three diets lowered blood pressure and also lowered Low Density Lipoprotein (LDL), the "bad" cholesterol. (More on this later in this section.)

2. Healthy Weight Management

DASH can help you maintain a healthy weight because it's high in fiber and well balanced for all nutrients. Fiber helps keep you full longer, and when you balance your plate at meals with low-fat protein and healthy fats, you won't get hungry as quickly. Also, when you begin to balance your meals, you'll have fewer cravings. As you may know, the calories from sugar and sweets quickly add up. Since sugar is reduced with DASH, the meal plan can potentially result in weight loss.

3. Lower Levels of Bad Cholesterol

DASH can control or lower the levels of "bad" cholesterol, a.k.a. LDL cholesterol. A healthy LDL should be less than 100, but you should check with your doctor to determine your overall risk. DASH likely lowers LDL because the plan is low in saturated fat. Fiber also helps lower blood cholesterol levels, so the added whole grains, beans, vegetables, and fruits are all good!

4. Lower Risk/Control Type 2 Diabetes

DASH may also help lower the risk of type 2 diabetes. Since the diet is balanced and low in sugar, it's a good choice for anyone with diabetes. Since fruit is higher in sugar than vegetables, it's best to meet your fruit/veggie goals by including more vegetables. Aim for 5 to 6 servings of vegetables and 2 to 3 servings of fruit per day.

1. Foods to Eat

The DASH diet focuses on eating heart-healthy foods that you can find in your grocery store. These foods are naturally high in fiber, magnesium, potassium and calcium. They're also low in sodium.

If you follow the DASH diet, you'll eat plenty of:

- Fruits.

- Vegetables.

- Whole grains.

- Nuts, seeds and legumes.

- Low-fat dairy.

2. Foods to Minimize

DASH also encourages you to cut back on foods that can raise your blood pressure. These include:

- Fatty meats, such as red meat and poultry with the skin on.

- Full-fat dairy, such as whole milk, cream and butter.

- Oils that are solid at room temperature, such as coconut and palm oils.

- High-sugar foods like candy, baked goods and desserts.

- High-sugar drinks, such as soda, juice and sweetened coffee or tea.

If you follow DASH, you don't have to eliminate these foods, says Patton. Instead, take steps toward healthier choices each day. The plan will be easier to stick with. For instance, consider replacing a meat entrée with a meatless option once a week.

Most Americans eat more meat than necessary at the expense of their vegetable intake. DASH recommends consuming no more than 6 ounces of meat per day. In its place, eat more fruits and veggies, which contain disease-fighting antioxidants, fiber and other nutrients.

1. Don't do everything at once. Major changes take time, and if you keep this in mind, you are more likely to be successful with your new dietary lifestyle. Begin by making one or two small changes at a time, and keep with them until they begin to feel natural, before making more changes. For example, switch to lower fat dairy this week and work on adding more produce next week. Gradually increase servings of those fresh fruits and vegetables by adding one serving to one meal a day, for example. Not only will making these changes gradually be good for your mental commitment, it will help your body adjust to the increase in fiber and the slight detoxification you get from eliminating processed foods and extra sodium.

2. Familiarize yourself with portion sizes. You'll learn that one serving of meat is three to four ounces, and that you need to consume four to five servings of vegetables, but do you really understand what that looks like, and how consuming those amounts of foods will make you feel in terms of satiety? Understanding what portion sizes look and feel like will go a long way in helping you follow DASH Diet guidelines.

3. Beware of condiments and sauces as these are often heavy in salt, sugar, and fats. Even the most unassuming ones — such as ketchup — can add milligrams of salt and unwanted sugar to your diet. Ask for foods to be prepared without extra sauces or have them served on the side so that you are in charge of how much you consume.

4. Always read labels. Always. Pay particular attention to saturated fat, sodium, and fiber content. When something appears to be high in sodium or fats, weigh what you will be giving up against what you gain from one portion of that food and ask yourself if it is worth it. In some cases, you may feel that it is. In others, the idea of giving up several servings of other foods for just one of this food will be enough to persuade you to put it down and move on to something else.

5. Don't be afraid to modify your recipes. DASH isn't about putting your favorites away forever; it is about modifying them so that you can still enjoy them whenever you want without worrying that you are damaging your health. Make lower fat substitutions, reduce the amount of meat while increasing the number of grains or vegetables, and reduce the amount of sugar and salt while making ingredient choices that enhance the flavor. For instance, add sugar-free applesauce to reduce the sugar content in a muffin recipe, or a nice spice blend to help you forget that you hardly used any salt in your treasured stew recipe.

6. Look at new ways of preparing foods. If you love fried foods, you can try oven frying those foods using olive oil and whole wheat breading. Consider using low sodium broth instead of heavy oils for sautéing and learn how to steam, bake and sauté your favorite foods. These preparations are not only healthier; they are easy and require little cleanup.

7. Never allow yourself to go hungry, because when you are hungry you are more likely to indulge in the very foods you are trying to cut out of your life. If you find that you are hungry immediately after a meal, then your portions are too small, and you should bulk up your meals a little bit. Keep plenty of fresh snacks available to help curb hunger between meals.

9. Never go to the grocery store hungry. Either do your grocery shopping after a meal, or keep a healthy snack (such as fruit or vegetables) in your car to nibble before you go in. If you are not hungry, you are more likely to stick with your dietary plan rather than splurging on things that provide you with no nutrition and too much salt and fat.

10. Choose fresh whenever possible. When fresh produce is an option, choose it over canned. Frozen produce is also an excellent option as there is not the same sodium content as in canned goods. Speaking of frozen foods, limit your choices to frozen vegetables and fruits while staying away from frozen prepared meals and snacks. If you are really craving those frozen jalapeno peppers, make your own by stuffing fresh peppers with low-fat cheese and spices. There is a healthy alternative to just about everything; there is no need to depend on the frozen food section for your favorite snacks and meals.

Chives and sesame omelet

Servings:4

Cooking time: 15 minutes

Ingredients:

- 4 eggs, whisked
- 1 tablespoon avocado oil
- 1 teaspoon sesame seeds
- 1 tablespoon chives, chopped
- ¼ cup low-fat milk

Directions:

1. Heat up avocado oil in the pan.
2. Mix up eggs and milk and pour the liquid in the skillet.
3. Add chives and sesame seeds.
4. Cook the omelet for 7 minutes.
5. Flip the omelet and cook it for 6 minutes more over the low heat.

Nutrition Info:

- 79 calories, 6.2g protein, 1.5g carbohydrates, 5.3g fat, 0.3g fiber, 164mg cholesterol, 69mg sodium, 99mg potassium.

Servings:4

Cooking time: 15 minutes

Ingredients:

- 4 eggs, beaten
- 1 tablespoon margarine
- 1 cup bell peppers, chopped
- 2 oz scallions, chopped

Directions:

1. Toss the margarine in the skillet and melt it.
2. In the mixing bowl mix up eggs and bell peppers. Add scallions.
3. Pour the egg mixture in the hot skillet and roast the omelet for 12 minutes.

Nutrition Info:

- 102 calories, 6.1g protein, 3.7g carbohydrates, 7.3g fat, 0.8g fiber, 164mg cholesterol, 98mg sodium, 156mg potassium.

Cheese hash browns

Servings:6

Cooking time: 30 minutes

Ingredients:

- 1 teaspoon olive oil
- 3 eggs, beaten
- 2 cups hash browns
- 3 oz vegan mozzarella, shredded

Directions:

1. Heat up olive oil and add hash browns.
2. Roast them for 5 minutes. Stir occasionally.
3. After this, pour eggs over hash browns and transfer the meal in the preheated to 380f oven.
4. Bake the meal for 20 minutes.

Nutrition Info:

- 211 calories, 4.8g protein, 21.9g carbohydrates, 12.5g fat, 1.7g fiber, 82mg cholesterol, 314mg sodium, 329mg potassium.

Servings:3

Cooking time: 5 minutes

Ingredients:

- 3 eggs
- 3 whole-grain bread slices
- 1 teaspoon olive oil
- ¼ teaspoon minced garlic
- ¼ teaspoon ground black pepper

Directions:

1. Heat up olive oil in the skillet.
2. Crack the eggs inside and cook them for 4 minutes.
3. Meanwhile, rub the bread slices with minced garlic.
4. Top the bread with cooked eggs and sprinkle with ground black pepper.

Nutrition Info:

- 157 calories,8.6g protein, 13.5g carbohydrates, 7.4g fat, 2.1g fiber, 164mg cholesterol, 182mg sodium, 62mg potassium.

Curry tofu scramble

Servings:3

Cooking time: 5 minutes

Ingredients:

- 12 oz tofu, crumbled
- 1 teaspoon curry powder
- ¼ cup skim milk
- 1 teaspoon olive oil
- ¼ teaspoon chili flakes

Directions:

1. Heat up olive oil in the skillet.
2. Add crumbled tofu and chili flakes.
3. In the bowl mix up curry powder and skim milk.
4. Pour the liquid over the crumbled tofu and stir well.
5. Cook the scrambled tofu for 3 minutes on the medium-high heat.

Nutrition Info:

- 102 calories, 10g protein, 3.3g carbohydrates, 6.4g fat, 1.2g fiber, 0mg cholesterol, 25mg sodium, 210mg potassium.

Servings:4
Cooking time: 25 minutes

Ingredients:

- 1 cup wild rice
- 1.5 cup low-fat milk
- 1 tablespoon vanilla extract
- 1 oz walnuts, chopped
- ¼ cup of soy milk

Directions:

1. Put all ingredients in the pan and close the lid.
2. Simmer the meal for 25 minutes.

Nutrition Info:

- 269 calories, 8.6g protein, 43.6g carbohydrates, 5.7g fat, 1.2g fiber, 5mg cholesterol, 51g sodium, 250mg potassium.

Fruits and rice pudding

Servings:3
Cooking time: 10 minutes

Ingredients:

- ½ cup long-grain rice
- 1 ½ cup low-fat milk
- 1 teaspoon vanilla extract
- 2 oz apricots, chopped

Directions:

1. Pour milk and add rice in the saucepan.
2. Close the lid and cook the rice on the medium-high heat for 10 minutes.
3. Then add vanilla extract and stir the rice well.
4. Transfer the pudding in the bowls and top with apricots.

Nutrition Info:

- 171 calories,6.4g protein, 32.9g carbohydrates, 0.3g fat, 0.8g fiber, 2mg cholesterol, 67mg sodium, 276mg potassium.

Servings:3

Cooking time: 5 minutes

Ingredients:

- 3 whole-grain bread slices
- 1 teaspoon vanilla extract
- 1 egg, beaten
- 2 tablespoons low-fat sour cream
- 1 tablespoon margarine

Directions:

1. Melt the butter in the skillet.
2. Meanwhile, in the bowl mix up vanilla extract, eggs, and low-fat sour cream.
3. Dip the bread slices in the egg mixture well.
4. Then transfer them in the melted margarine and roast for 2 minutes from each side.

Nutrition Info:

- 166 calories,5.1g protein, 18.7g carbohydrates, 7.9g fat, 2g fiber, 58mg cholesterol, 229mg sodium, 39mg potassium.

Blueberries mix

Servings:4

Cooking time: 0 minutes

Ingredients:

- 1 cups oats
- 4 tablespoons chia seeds
- 2 cups of coconut milk
- 1 cup blueberries

Directions:

1. Mix up all ingredients together and transfer them in the serving glasses.
2. Refrigerate the meal for 8 hours.

Nutrition Info:

- 443 calories, 8.1g protein, 31.7g carbohydrates, 34.4g fat, 10.5g fiber, 0mg cholesterol, 22mg sodium, 475mg potassium.

Servings:1

Cooking time: 0 minutes

Ingredients:

- 1/3 cup low-fat yogurt
- 1 teaspoon almond flakes
- 1 fresh fig, chopped
- 1 teaspoon liquid honey
- ¼ teaspoon sesame seeds

Directions:

1. Mix up yogurt and honey and pour the mixture in the serving glass.
2. Top it with chopped fig, almond flakes, and sesame seeds.

Nutrition Info:

- 178 calories,6.2g protein, 24.4g carbohydrates, 6.8g fat, 3.1g fiber, 5mg cholesterol, 44mg sodium, 283mg potassium.

Strawberry sandwich

Servings:4

Cooking time: 0 minutes

Ingredients:

- 4 tablespoons low-fat yogurt
- 4 strawberries, sliced
- 4 whole-wheat bread slices

Directions:

1. Spread the bread with yogurt and then top with sliced strawberries.

Nutrition Info:

- 84 calories, 4.6g protein, 13.6g carbohydrates, 1.2g fat, 2.1g fiber, 1mg cholesterol, 143mg sodium, 124mg potassium.

Servings:12
Cooking time: 10 minutes
Ingredients:

- 1 cup almond flour
- 1 cups low-fat milk
- 1 teaspoon margarine
- 1 teaspoon baking powder
- 3 tablespoons whole-wheat flour

Directions:

1. In a bowl, mix up all the flour with, milk, and baking powder, and whisk well.
2. Heat up a pan with the margarine over medium heat, add ¼ cup of the crepes batter, spread into the pan, cook for 1-2 minutes per side.
3. Repeat the steps with the remaining batter.

Nutrition Info:

- 32 calories, 1.4g protein, 3.2g carbohydrates, 1.7g fat, 0.3g fiber, 1mg cholesterol, 14mg sodium, 75mg potassium.

Bean frittata

Servings:4
Cooking time: 12 minutes
Ingredients:

- 4 eggs, beaten
- ½ cup red kidney beans, canned
- ½ onion, diced
- 1 tablespoon margarine
- 1 teaspoon dried dill

Directions:

1. Toss the margarine in the skillet. Add onion and saute it for 4 minutes or until it is soft.
2. Then add red kidney beans and dried dill. Mix the mixture up.
3. Pour the eggs over it and close the lid.
4. Cook the frittata on medium-low heat for 7 minutes or until it is set or bake it in the oven at 390f for 5 minutes.

Nutrition Info:

- 172 calories, 11g protein, 15.9g carbohydrates, 7.5g fat, 3.8g fiber, 164mg cholesterol, 99mg sodium, 401mg potassium.

Servings:8

Cooking time: 30 minutes

Ingredients:

- 5 eggs, beaten
- ½ cup bell pepper, chopped
- 1 cup red kidney beans, cooked
- ½ cup white onions, chopped
- 1 cup low-fat mozzarella cheese, shredded

Directions:

1. Spread the beans over the casserole mold. Add onions and bell pepper.
2. Add the eggs mixed with the cheese.
3. Bake the casserole 380 f for 30 minutes.

Nutrition Info:

- 142 calories, 12.8g protein, 16g carbohydrates, 3g fat, 4.3g fiber, 105mg cholesterol, 162mg sodium, 374mg potassium.

Grape yogurt

Servings:3

Cooking time: 0 minutes

Ingredients:

- 1 ½ cup low-fat yogurt
- ½ cup grapes, chopped
- 1 oz walnuts, chopped

Directions:

1. Mix up all ingredients together and transfer them in the serving glasses.

Nutrition Info:

- 156 calories, 9.4g protein, 12.2g carbohydrates, 7.1g fat, 0.8g fiber, 7mg cholesterol, 86mg sodium, 365mg potassium.

Servings:4

Cooking time: 25 minutes

Ingredients:

- 1 cup low-fat milk
- 1 cup wild rice
- ½ teaspoon vanilla extract
- ¼ cup cherries, pitted and halved

Directions:

1. Put the milk in a pot and add rice.
2. Simmer the mixture for 25 minutes stirring often.
3. Add all remaining ingredients and mix up well.

Nutrition Info:

- 201 calories, 5.4g protein, 41.4g carbohydrates, 0.9g fat, 0.6g fiber, 3mg cholesterol, 30mg sodium, 150mg potassium.

Whole grain pancakes

Servings:4

Cooking time: 10 minutes

Ingredients:

- ½ teaspoon baking powder
- ¼ cup skim milk
- 1 cup whole-grain wheat flour
- 2 teaspoons liquid honey
- 1 teaspoon olive oil

Directions:

1. Mix up baking powder and flour in the bowl.
2. Add skim milk and olive oil. Whisk the mixture well.
3. Preheat the non-stick skillet and pour the small amount of dough inside in the shape of the pancake. Cook it for 2 minutes from each side or until the pancake is golden brown.
4. Top the cooked pancakes with liquid honey.

Nutrition Info:

- 129 calories,4.6g protein, 25.7g carbohydrates, 1.7g fat, 3.7g fiber, 0mg cholesterol, 10mg sodium, 211mg potassium.

Servings:3
Cooking time: 2 minutes
Ingredients:

- ½ cup almonds, chopped
- 1 cup low-fat milk
- 1 banana, peeled, chopped

Directions:

1. Put all ingredients in the blender and blend until smooth.
2. Pour the smoothie in the serving glasses.

Nutrition Info:

- 161 calories,6.5g protein, 16.4g carbohydrates, 8.8g fat, 3g fiber, 4mg cholesterol, 36mg sodium, 379mg potassium.

Baked fruits

Servings:4
Cooking time: 10 minutes
Ingredients:

- 2 teaspoons liquid honey
- 1 teaspoon ground cinnamon
- 4 peaches, halved

Directions:

1. Grease a baking pan with the margarine and put the peaches inside. Sprinkle them with ground cinnamon.
2. Bake peaches at 360f for 10 minutes and then sprinkle with honey.

Nutrition Info:

- 71 calories, 1.4g protein, 17.4g carbohydrates, 0.4g fat, 2.6g fiber, 0mg cholesterol, 0mg sodium, 289mg potassium.

Servings:1
Cooking time: 0 minutes
Ingredients:

- 1 tablespoon chia seeds
- ½ cup low-fat milk, hot
- 1 teaspoon margarine
- 1 teaspoon liquid honey
- ½ cup oatmeal

Directions:

1. In the glass jar mix up all ingredients and close the lid.
2. Let the meal rest for 6 hours in chill place.

Nutrition Info:

- 33 4calories, 12g protein, 45.9g carbohydrates, 12.2g fat, 9.3g fiber, 6mg cholesterol, 103mg sodium, 398mg potassium.

Millet cream

Servings:4
Cooking time: 30 minutes
Ingredients:

- 14 ounces low-fat milk
- 1 cup millet
- 1 teaspoon liquid honey
- ½ teaspoon vanilla extract

Directions:

1. Put the milk in a pot, bring to a simmer over medium heat, add the millet and the vanilla extract, and cook for 30 minutes stirring often.
2. Top the cooked millet cream with honey.

Nutrition Info:

- 989 calories, 5.9g protein, 37.9g carbohydrates, 2.1g fat, 4.3g fiber, 0mg cholesterol, 189mg sodium, 99mg potassium.

Servings:4
Cooking time: 8 minutes
Ingredients:

- 4 tomatoes, chopped
- 1 teaspoon margarine
- 1 teaspoon italian seasonings
- 4 egg whites

Directions:

1. Heat up margarine in the skillet.
2. Add italian seasonings and tomatoes and saute the mixture for 5 minutes.
3. Then add egg whites and whisk it well.
4. Cook the meal for 5 minutes over the low heat.

Nutrition Info:

- 51 calories, 4.7g protein, 5.2g carbohydrates, 1.6g fat, 1.5g fiber, 1mg cholesterol, 51mg sodium, 346mg potassium.

Dill omelet

Servings:6
Cooking time: 6 minutes
Ingredients:

- 2 tablespoons low-fat milk
- ¼ teaspoon white pepper
- 6 eggs, beaten
- 2 tablespoons dill, chopped
- 1 tablespoon avocado oil

Directions:

1. Heat up avocado oil in the skillet.
2. In a bowl, mix up all ingredients.
3. Pour the egg mixture in the hot oil and cook the omelet for 6 minutes.

Nutrition Info:

- 71 calories, 6g protein, 1.4g carbohydrates, 4.8g fat, 0.3g fiber, 164mg cholesterol, 66mg sodium, 109mg potassium.

Tomato brussel sprouts

Servings:4
Cooking time: 25 minutes
Ingredients:

- 1 tablespoon olive oil
- 1 pound brussels sprouts, trimmed and halved
- 1 tablespoon tomato sauce

Directions:

1. In a baking dish, combine the sprouts with the oil and tomato sauce.
2. Bake the vegetables at 400f for 25 minutes.

Nutrition Info:

- 80 calories, 3.9g protein, 10.5g carbohydrates, 3.9g fat, 4.3g fiber, 0mg cholesterol, 48mg sodium, 453mg potassium.

Milky mash

Servings:4
Cooking time: 25 minutes
Ingredients:

- 2 pounds cauliflower florets
- ¼ cup low-fat milk
- 1 teaspoon spinach, blended
- 2 cups of water

Directions:

1. Mix up water and cauliflower in the pan and cook the vegetables for 25 minutes. Drain the cauliflower.
2. Mash the cauliflower, add milk and spinach.

Nutrition Info:

- 63 calories, 5g protein, 12.8g carbohydrates, 0.4g fat, 5.7g fiber, 1mg cholesterol, 78mg sodium, 712 potassium.

Servings:4
Cooking time: 15 minutes

Ingredients:

- 1 cup corn kernels
- 2 oz basil, chopped
- 1 tablespoon olive oil
- 1 yellow onion, chopped
- ½ teaspoon red pepper flakes

Directions:

1. Heat up a pan with the oil over medium-high heat, add the onion, stir and sauté for 5 minutes.
2. Then add all remaining ingredients, stir well and cook for 10 minutes more over the medium heat.

Nutrition Info:

- 78 calories, 2g protein, 10.3g carbohydrates, 4.1g fat, 1.9g fiber, 0mg cholesterol, 7mg sodium, 191mg potassium.

Fried zucchini

Servings:4
Cooking time: 20 minutes

Ingredients:

- 4 zucchinis, cut into fries
- ½ teaspoon ground black pepper
- 1 tablespoon olive oil
- ¼ teaspoon onion powder

Directions:

1. Line the baking tray with baking paper and arrange the zucchini inside.
2. Sprinkle them with ground black pepper, olive oil, and onion powder.
3. Bake the vegetables at 400f for 20 minutes.

Nutrition Info:

- 63 calories, 2.4g protein, 6.9g carbohydrates, 3.9g fat, 2.2g fiber, 0mg cholesterol, 20mg sodium, 518mg potassium.

Servings:4

Cooking time: 6 minutes

Ingredients:

- 2 pounds asparagus, trimmed
- 2 tablespoons canola oil
- 1 teaspoon dried sage

Directions:

1. Mix up asparagus, oil, and sage.
2. Transfer the vegetables in the grill and cook for 3 minutes at 400 f.

Nutrition Info:

- 108 calories, 5g protein, 8.9g carbohydrates, 7.3g fat, 4.8g fiber, 0mg cholesterol, 5mg sodium, 460mg potassium.

Quinoa bowl

Servings:5

Cooking time: 7 minutes

Ingredients:

- 1 cup quinoa
- 2 cups of water
- 1 avocado, sliced
- 1 teaspoon cayenne pepper
- 1 tablespoon margarine

Directions:

1. Pour water in the saucepan.
2. Add quinoa and cook it for 7 minutes.
3. Then add margarine and cayenne pepper. Stir the quinoa well.
4. Transfer it in the serving bowls and top with sliced avocado.

Nutrition Info:

- 229 calories,5.6g protein, 25.5g carbohydrates, 12.2g fat, 5.2g fiber, 0mg cholesterol, 34mg sodium, 396mg potassium.

Servings:6
Cooking time: 20 minutes
Ingredients:

- 3 pounds potatoes, chopped
- 1 cup of water
- 3 tablespoons low-fat sour cream

Directions:

1. Boil the potatoes in water for 20 minutes and then drain.
2. Mash the potatoes and mix up with low-fat sour cream.

Nutrition Info:

- 169 calories, 4g protein, 35.9g carbohydrates, 1.5g fat, 5.4g fiber, 3mg cholesterol, 18mg sodium, 932mg potassium.

Spiced baby carrot

Servings:4
Cooking time: 30 minutes
Ingredients:

- 1 pound baby carrots, trimmed
- 1 tablespoon smoked paprika
- 1 teaspoon lemon juice
- 3 tablespoons avocado oil

Directions:

1. Arrange the carrots on a lined baking sheet.
2. Sprinkle the vegetables with all remaining ingredients and bake at 390f for 30 minutes.

Nutrition Info:

- 59 calories, 1.1g protein, 10.9g carbohydrates, 1.7g fat, 4.4g fiber, 0mg cholesterol, 90mg sodium, 344mg potassium.

Servings:4

Cooking time: 30 minutes

Ingredients:

- 2 pounds cremini mushrooms, halved
- 2 tablespoons olive oil
- 1 tablespoon thyme, chopped
- 2 tablespoons cilantro, chopped
- ¼ teaspoon ground black pepper

Directions:

1. Mix up all ingredients and transfer them in the baking tray.
2. Cook the mushrooms at 400f for 30 minutes.

Nutrition Info:

- 124 calories, 5.8g protein, 9.9g carbohydrates, 7.3g fat, 1.7g fiber, 0mg cholesterol, 14mg sodium, 1026mg potassium

Asparagus in sauce

Servings:4

Cooking time: 20 minutes

Ingredients:

- 1-pound asparagus, chopped
- 2 tablespoons garlic sauce
- 1 tablespoon margarine, melted

Directions:

1. Put the asparagus in the tray and sprinkle with garlic sauce and melted margarine.
2. Cook the vegetables at 400f for 20 minutes.

Nutrition Info:

- 51 calories, 2.6g protein, 4.9g carbohydrates, 3g fat, 2.4g fiber, 0mg cholesterol, 50mg sodium, 231mg potassium.2

Servings:4

Cooking time: 30 minutes

Ingredients:

- 2 tablespoons olive oil
- 1 pound carrots, peeled and roughly cubed
- 1 white onion, chopped
- 1 tablespoon sweet paprika

Directions:

1. Put the carrot in the baking tray, add all remaining ingredients and shale well.
2. Bake the carrots at 380f for 30 minutes.

Nutrition Info:

- 122 calories, 1.5g protein, 14.7g carbohydrates, 7.3g fat, 4g fiber, 0mg cholesterol, 80mg sodium, 443mg potassium.

Cauliflower bake

Servings:4

Cooking time: 30 minutes

Ingredients:

- 2 tablespoons chili sauce
- 3 garlic cloves, minced
- 1 cauliflower head, florets separated
- 1 teaspoon margarine
- ½ cup low-fat milk

Directions:

1. Mix up all ingredients in the baking pan.
2. Cook the meal at 400 degrees f for 30 minutes.

Nutrition Info:

- 42 calories, 2.5g protein, 5.9g carbohydrates, 1.4g fat, 1.7g fiber, 2mg cholesterol, 235mg sodium, 266mg potassium.

Servings:4

Cooking time: 30 minutes

Ingredients:

- 2 pounds carrots, halved
- ½ teaspoon dried cilantro
- 3 tablespoons olive oil

Directions:

1. Put the carrots in the baking pan, sprinkle with olive oil and dried cilantro.
2. Bake the carrots at 390f for 25 minutes.

Nutrition Info:

- 183 calories, 1.9g protein, 22.3g carbohydrates, 10.5g fat, 5.6g fiber, 0mg cholesterol, 156mg sodium, 725mg potassium.

Beans in blended spinach

Servings:4

Cooking time: 15 minutes

Ingredients:

- ½ cup fresh spinach, blended
- 2 teaspoons smoked paprika
- 2 cups green beans, chopped
- 1 tablespoon lime juice
- 2 tablespoons avocado oil

Directions:

1. Heat up a pan with the oil over medium-high heat.
2. Add the beans and all the remaining ingredients.
3. Cook them for 15 minutes over the medium heat.

Nutrition Info:

- 31 calories, 1.4g protein, 5.3g carbohydrates, 1.1g fat, 2.7g fiber, 0mg cholesterol, 8mg sodium, 186mg potassium.

Servings:4

Cooking time: 20 minutes

Ingredients:

- 2 endives, halved lengthwise
- 2 tablespoons olive oil
- ½ teaspoon turmeric powder

Directions:

1. In a baking pan, combine the endives and all remaining ingredients.
2. Bake the meal at 400 f for 20 minutes.

Nutrition Info:

- 105 calories, 3.2g protein, 8.8g carbohydrates, 7.5g fat, 8g fiber, 0mg cholesterol, 57mg sodium, 812mg potassium.

Light corn stew

Servings:4

Cooking time: 12 minutes

Ingredients:

- 4 cups corn kernels
- 1 cup collard greens, chopped
- ½ teaspoon smoked paprika
- ¼ cup low-fat milk
- 3 oz scallions, chopped

Directions:

1. Put al ingredients in the saucepan, stir well, and close the lid.
2. Cook the stew for 12 minutes on the medium heat.

Nutrition Info:

- 149 calories, 6.2g protein, 32.1g carbohydrates, 2.1g fat, 5.2g fiber, 1mg cholesterol, 35mg sodium, 504mg potassium.

Servings:6

Cooking time: 18 minutes

Ingredients:

- 1-pound cauliflower florets
- 1 tablespoon curry powder
- ¼ cup of soy milk
- 1 tablespoon margarine
- ½ teaspoon dried oregano

Directions:

1. Preheat the oven to 375f.
2. After this, melt the margarine in the saucepan.
3. Mix up together soy milk and curry powder and whisk the liquid until smooth.
4. Then pour it in the saucepan with the melted margarine and bring to boil.
5. Add cauliflower florets and stir well.
6. Close the lid and cook the vegetables for 5 minutes. After this, transfer the saucepan in the preheated oven and cook the meal for 10 minutes or until the florets are soft.

Nutrition Info:

- 45calories, 2g protein, 5.4g carbohydrates, 2.3g fat, 2.4g fiber, 0mg cholesterol, 51mg sodium, 260mg potassium.

Grilled tomatoes

Servings:4

Cooking time: 2 minutes

Ingredients:

- 4 tomatoes
- ½ teaspoon dried basil
- 1 tablespoon olive oil
- ½ teaspoon dried oregano

Directions:

1. Preheat the grill to 390f.
2. Meanwhile, slice the tomatoes roughly and sprinkle with dried basil and dried oregano.
3. After this, sprinkle the vegetables with olive oil and place in the preheated grill.
4. Grill the tomatoes for 40 seconds from each side.

Nutrition Info:

- 53 calories,1.1g protein, 4.9g carbohydrates, 3.8g fat, 1.6g fiber, 0mg cholesterol, 6mg sodium, 295mg potassium.

Servings:8

Cooking time: 35 minutes

Ingredients:

- 8 potatoes, halved
- 2 tablespoons olive oil
- ½ teaspoon garlic powder
- 1 teaspoon dried thyme

Directions:

1. Rub the potatoes with garlic powder and thyme.
2. Then brush the potatoes with olive oil and transfer in the baking pan,
3. Bake the potatoes at 375f for 35 minutes.

Nutrition Info:

- 178 calories, 3.6g protein, 33.7g carbohydrates, 3.7g fat, 5.2g fiber, 0mg cholesterol, 13mg sodium, 870mg potassium.

Dijon potatoes

Servings:4

Cooking time: 60 minutes

Ingredients:

- 2 cups potatoes, peeled and cut into wedges
- 2 tablespoons olive oil
- 1 tablespoon dijon mustard
- 1 teaspoon minced garlic

Directions:

1. In a baking pan, combine the potatoes with all remaining ingredients and transfer in the preheated to 400f oven.
2. Bake the meal for 60 minutes.

Nutrition Info:

- 115 calories, 1.5g protein, 12.2g carbohydrates, 7.2g fat, 1.9g fiber, 0mg cholesterol, 49mg sodium, 313mg potassium.

Servings:6
Cooking time: 20 minutes
Ingredients:

- 2-pounds brussels sprouts, halved
- 1 tablespoon sesame oil
- 2 teaspoons apple cider vinegar
- 2 teaspoons chili sauce
- 1 tablespoon sesame seeds

Directions:

1. Put the brussel sprouts in the baking pan.
2. Sprinkle them with sesame oil, apple cider vinegar, and chili sauce.
3. Bake the vegetables at 400f for 20 minutes.
4. Sprinkle the cooked vegetables with sesame seeds.

Nutrition Info:

- 94 calories, 5.4g protein, 14.2g carbohydrates, 3.6g fat, 5.9g fiber, 0mg cholesterol, 80mg sodium, 598mg potassium.

Braised baby carrot

Servings:3
Cooking time: 22 minutes
Ingredients:

- 1 cup baby carrots
- 1 teaspoon dried thyme
- 1 tablespoon olive oil
- ½ cup vegetable stock
- 1 garlic clove, sliced

Directions:

1. Heat up olive oil in the saucepan for 30 seconds.
2. Then add sliced garlic and dried thyme. Bring the mixture boil and add the baby carrot.
3. Roast the vegetables for 7 minutes over the medium heat. Stir them constantly.
4. After this, add vegetable stock and close the lid.
5. Cook the baby carrots for 15 minutes or until they are tender.

Nutrition Info:

- 64 calories,0.6g protein, 5.6g carbohydrates, 4.8g fat, 1.9g fiber, 0mg cholesterol, 111mg sodium, 141mg potassium.

Servings:3

Cooking time: 20 minutes

Ingredients:

- 2 carrots, peeled
- 1 tablespoon avocado oil
- 1 teaspoon five spices powder
- 2 tablespoons water

Directions:

1. Rub the carrots with five spices powder and sprinkle with avocado oil.
2. Then transfer the vegetables in the tray and sprinkle with water.
3. Bake the carrots for 20 minutes at 375f or until they are tender.
4. Cut the cooked carrot into pieces.

Nutrition Info:

- 31 calories, 1g protein, 4.8g carbohydrates, 0.6g fat, 2.3g fiber, 0mg cholesterol, 28mg sodium, 145mg potassium.

Fragrant tomatoes

Servings:4

Cooking time: 20 minutes

Ingredients:

- 2 cups tomatoes, halved
- 1 tablespoon basil, chopped
- 3 tablespoons avocado oil
- 1 tablespoon lemon zest, grated
- ¼ cup low-fat parmesan, grated

Directions:

1. Mix up tomatoes, basil, avocado oil, and lemon zest in the tray.
2. Sprinkle the parmesan on top and bake the vegetables in the oven at 375 f for 20 minutes.

Nutrition Info:

- 48 calories, 2.2g protein, 4.5g carbohydrates, 2.8g fat, 1.6g fiber, 6mg cholesterol, 100mg sodium, 261mg potassium.

Servings:4
Cooking time: 30 minutes
Ingredients:

- 2 tablespoons olive oil
- 1 pound broccoli florets
- 1 tablespoon lime juice
- 3 tablespoons parsley, chopped

Directions:

1. Line the baking pan with baking paper.
2. Then put the broccoli inside and sprinkle the vegetables with lime juice, olive oil, and parsley.
3. Cover the broccoli with foil.
4. Bake the meal at 400f for 30 minutes.

Nutrition Info:

- 101 calories, 3.3g protein, 8.2g carbohydrates, 7.4g fat, 3.1g fiber, 0mg cholesterol, 40mg sodium, 380mg potassium.

Grinded corn

Servings:4
Cooking time: 15 minutes
Ingredients:

- 2 cups corn kernels, grinded
- 1 yellow onion, chopped
- ½ cup of soy milk
- 1 teaspoon cayenne pepper
- 1 teaspoon margarine

Directions:

1. Heat up a pan over medium-high heat, add margarine and melt it.
2. Add corn, onion, cayenne pepper and stir and cook for 8 minutes.
3. Add soy milk and cork kernels. Simmer the meal for 5 minutes on low heat.

Nutrition Info:

- 103 calories, 3.9g protein, 19.3g carbohydrates, 2.5g fat, 3g fiber, 0mg cholesterol, 39mg sodium, 294mg potassium.

Servings:6

Cooking time: 3 minutes

Ingredients:

- 1-pound pineapple, peeled
- 1 teaspoon honey
- 1 teaspoon olive oil

Directions:

1. Cut the pineapple into rings and put them in the plastic bag.
2. Add all remaining ingredients and shake the pineapple rings well.
3. After this, preheat the grill to 400f.
4. Put the pineapple rings in the grill and roast them for 1.5 minutes from each side.

Nutrition Info:

- 48 calories,0.4g protein, 10.9g carbohydrates, 0.9g fat, 1.1g fiber, 0mg cholesterol, 1mg sodium, 83mg potassium.

Vegan salad

Servings:4
Cooking time: 0 minutes
Ingredients:

- 1 pound firm tofu, drained and cubed
- 1 tablespoon olive oil
- 1 cup bell pepper, chopped
- 1 cup cucumbers, chopped
- ½ cup sorrel leaves, torn

Directions:

1. Put all ingredients in the serving bowl and stir well.

Nutrition Info:

- 123 calories,9.8g protein, 5.1g carbohydrates, 8.3g fat, 1.6g fiber, 0mg cholesterol, 15mg sodium, 262mg potassium.

Tender green beans salad

Servings:8
Cooking time: 0 minutes
Ingredients:

- 2 cups green beans, trimmed, chopped, cooked
- 2 tablespoons olive oil
- 2 pounds shrimp, cooked, peeled
- 1 cup tomato, chopped
- ¼ cup apple cider vinegar

Directions:

1. Mix up all ingredients together.
2. Then transfer the salad in the salad bowl.

Nutrition Info:

- 179 calories,26.5g protein, 4.6g carbohydrates, 5.5g fat, 1.2g fiber, 239mg cholesterol, 280mg sodium, 308mg potassium.

Servings:4

Cooking time: 0 minutes

Ingredients:

- 7 oz canned salmon, shredded
- 1 tablespoon lime juice
- 1 tablespoon low-fat yogurt
- 1 cup baby spinach, chopped
- 1 teaspoon capers, drained and chopped

Directions:

1. Mix up all ingredients together and transfer them in the salad bowl.

Nutrition Info:

- 71 calories,10.1g protein, 0.8g carbohydrates, 3.2g fat, 0.2g fiber, 22mg cholesterol, 52mg sodium, 244mg potassium.

Salad skewers

Servings:4

Cooking time: 0 minutes

Ingredients:

- 2 cucumbers
- 2 cups cherry tomatoes
- ½ teaspoon lemon juice
- 1 teaspoon olive oil

Directions:

1. Cut the cucumbers on medium cubes.
2. Then string the cucumber cubes and cherry tomatoes into skewers one-by-one.
3. Then sprinkle the salad skewers with lemon juice and olive oil.

Nutrition Info:

- 49 calories, 1.8g protein, 9g carbohydrates, 1.5g fat, 1.8g fiber, 0mg cholesterol, 8mg sodium, 435mg potassium.

Servings:4

Cooking time: 0 minutes

Ingredients:

- 2 fennel bulbs, chopped
- 1 cup fresh parsley, chopped
- 1 tablespoon olive oil
- ½ cups walnuts, chopped
- 1 oz low-fat feta cheese, crumbled

Directions:

1. Put all ingredients in the salad bowl.
2. Mix up the mixture.

Nutrition Info:

- 181 calories,6.9g protein, 11.3g carbohydrates, 13.8g fat, 5.2g fiber, 3mg cholesterol, 156mg sodium, 649mg potassium.

Watercress salad

Servings:4

Cooking time: 4 minutes

Ingredients:

- 2 cups asparagus, chopped
- 16 ounces shrimp, cooked
- 4 cups watercress, torn
- 1 tablespoon apple cider vinegar
- ¼ cup olive oil

Directions:

1. In the mixing bowl mix up asparagus, shrimps, watercress, and olive oil.
2. T

Nutrition Info:

- 264 calories,28.3g protein, 4.5g carbohydrates, 14.8g fat, 1.8g fiber, 239mg cholesterol, 300mg sodium, 393mg potassium.

Servings:4

Cooking time: 0 minutes

Ingredients:

- 1 cup mango, peeled and cubed
- 2 cups oranges, chopped
- 1 tablespoon low-fat yogurt
- 2 tablespoons walnuts, chopped
- 1 teaspoon vanilla extract

Directions:

1. Put all ingredients in the bowl and mix up well.
2. Then transfer the salad in the serving bowls.

Nutrition Info:

- 97 calories,2.4g protein, 17.6g carbohydrates, 2.6g fat, 3.1g fiber, 0g cholesterol, 3mg sodium, 263mg potassium.

Pine nuts salad

Servings:4

Cooking time: 0 minutes

Ingredients:

- 5 cups baby arugula
- 2 tablespoons chives, chopped
- 1 tablespoon balsamic vinegar
- 2 tablespoons avocado oil
- 3 tablespoons pine nuts

Directions:

1. Combine together all ingredients in the salad bowl and cool in the fridge for 3 minutes.

Nutrition Info:

- 60 calories,1.7g protein, 2.2g carbohydrates, 5.5g fat, 1g fiber, 0mg cholesterol, 7mg sodium, 160mg potassium.

Servings:4

Cooking time: 0 minutes

Ingredients:

- 8 oz beef sirloin, cooked, shredded
- 1 tablespoon mustard
- 1 bell pepper, sliced
- 2 cups lettuce, chopped
- 1 teaspoon lime juice

Directions:

1. In the salad bowl mix up bell pepper, lettuce, and shredded beef sirloin.
2. Sprinkle the salad with lime juice and mustard. Shake it.

Nutrition Info:

- 133 calories,18.3g protein, 4.3g carbohydrates, 4.5g fat, 1g fiber, 51mg cholesterol, 40mg sodium, 345mg potassium.

Seafood salad with grapes

Servings:4

Cooking time: 0 minutes

Ingredients:

- 2 tablespoons low-fat mayonnaise
- 2 teaspoons chili powder
- 1-pound shrimp, cooked, peeled
- 1 cup green grapes, halved
- 1 oz nuts, chopped

Directions:

1. Mix up all ingredients in the mixing bowl and transfer the salad in the serving plates.

Nutrition Info:

- 225 calories,27.4g protein, 9.9g carbohydrates, 8.3g fat, 1.3g fiber, 241mg cholesterol, 390mg sodium, 304mg potassium.

Servings:4

Cooking time: 0 minutes

Ingredients:

- 2 heads endives, chopped
- 1 tablespoon parsley, chopped
- 2 tablespoons lemon juice
- 2 tablespoons olive oil
- 2 cups arugula, chopped

Directions:

1. Put all ingredients from the list above in the salad bowl and stir well.

Nutrition Info:

- 108 calories,3.6g protein, 9.2g carbohydrates, 7.7g fat, 8.2g fiber, 0mg cholesterol, 61mg sodium, 857mg potassium.

Smoked salad

Servings:6

Cooking time: 0 minutes

Ingredients:

- 1 mango, chopped
- 4 cups lettuce, chopped
- 8 oz smoked turkey, chopped
- 2 tablespoons low-fat yogurt
- 1 teaspoon smoked paprika

Directions:

1. Mix up all ingredients in the bowls and transfer them in the serving plates.

Nutrition Info:

- 88 calories,7.1g protein, 11.2g carbohydrates, 1.9g fat, 1.3g fiber, 25mg cholesterol, 350mg sodium, 262mg potassium.

Servings:3

Cooking time: 0 minutes

Ingredients:

- 1 cup corn kernels, cooked
- 1 teaspoon low-fat sour cream
- 1 cup fresh spinach, chopped
- ½ cup celery stalk, chopped

Directions:

1. Mix up corn kernels, spinach, and celery stalk in the salad bowl.
2. Then sprinkle the cooked salad with low-fat sour cream.

Nutrition Info:

- 52 calories, 2.1g protein, 10.6g carbohydrates, 1g fat, 1.9g fiber, 1mg cholesterol, 30mg sodium, 240mg potassium.

Spring salad

Servings:4

Cooking time: 0 minutes

Ingredients:

- 3 oz scallions, chopped
- 1 tablespoon chives, chopped
- 3 cups radish, sliced
- 1 tablespoon low-fat yogurt
- ½ teaspoon ground black pepper

Directions:

1. Put all ingredients in the salad bowl and mix it up.

Nutrition Info:

- 24 calories,1.3g protein, 5g carbohydrates, 0.2g fat, 2g fiber, 0mg cholesterol, 40mg sodium, 276mg potassium.

Servings:4

Cooking time: 30 minutes

Ingredients:

- 2 cups pineapple, chopped
- 4 potatoes, cubed
- 1 tablespoon olive oil
- 1/3 cup almonds, chopped
- 2 tablespoons low-fat cream cheese

Directions:

1. Bake potatoes at 390f for 30 minutes or until soft.
2. Then mix up cooked potatoes with pineapple, olive oil, almonds, and cream cheese.

Nutrition Info:

- 281 calories,6.1g protein, 46.1g carbohydrates, 9.5g fat, 7.3g fiber, 6mg cholesterol, 29mg sodium, 1021mg potassium.

Bean sprouts salad

Servings:4

Cooking time: 0 minutes

Ingredients:

- 2 cups bean sprouts
- ½ cup bell pepper, chopped
- 1 tablespoon olive oil
- ½ cup cilantro, chopped
- 2 pecans, chopped

Directions:

1. Put all ingredients in the salad bowl and mix it up.

Nutrition Info:

- 111 calories,4.8g protein, 6g carbohydrates, 9g fat, 1g fiber, 0mg cholesterol, 7mg sodium, 239mg potassium.

Servings:4

Cooking time: 0 minutes

Ingredients:

- ½ cup low-fat greek yogurt
- 8 oz tuna, canned
- ½ cup fresh parsley, chopped
- 1 cup corn kernels, cooked
- ½ teaspoon ground black pepper

Directions:

1. Mix up tuna, parsley, kernels, and ground black pepper.
2. Then add yogurt and stir the salad until it is homogenous.

Nutrition Info:

- 172 calories,17.8g protein, 13.6g carbohydrates, 5.5g fat, 1.4g fiber, 19mg cholesterol, 55mg sodium, 392mg potassium.

Garlic edamame salad

Servings:4

Cooking time: 0 minutes

Ingredients:

- 2 tablespoons avocado oil
- 2 tablespoons apple cider vinegar
- 1 teaspoon minced garlic
- 2 cups edamame, cooked
- 2 tablespoons scallions, chopped

Directions:

1. Stir together all ingredients in the salad bowl.
2. Cool aside the salad for 5 minutes.

Nutrition Info:

- 201 calories,16.8g protein, 15.1g carbohydrates, 9.6g fat, 5.8g fiber, 0mg cholesterol, 20mg sodium, 832mg potassium.

Servings:3
Cooking time: 0 minutes

Ingredients:

- 2 cups lettuce, chopped
- 2 cups cucumbers, chopped
- ¼ cup balsamic vinegar
- 1 teaspoon mustard
- 1 teaspoon olive oil

Directions:

1. Make the dressing: Mix mustard, olive oil, and balsamic vinegar.
2. Then mix up lettuce and cucumbers in the salad bowl.
3. Top the salad with dressing and shake well.

Nutrition Info:

- 38 calories,0.9g protein, 4.2g carbohydrates, 2g fat, 0.7g fiber, 0mg cholesterol, 4mg sodium, 176mg potassium.

Cucumber and lettuce salad

Servings:4
Cooking time: 0 minutes

Ingredients:

- 2 cups romaine lettuce, roughly chopped
- 1 cup corn kernels, cooked
- ½ pound green beans, cooked, roughly chopped
- 1 cup cucumber, chopped
- 1 tablespoon canola oil

Directions:

1. Mix up all ingredients in the salad bowl and transfer the salad in the serving plates, if desired.

Nutrition Info:

- 89 calories,2.6g protein, 13.1g carbohydrates, 4.1g fat, 3.3g fiber, 0mg cholesterol, 11mg sodium, 300mg potassium.

Cauliflower steaks

Servings:4
Cooking time: 25 minutes
Ingredients:
- 1-pound cauliflower head
- 1 teaspoon ground turmeric
- ½ teaspoon cayenne pepper
- 2 tablespoons olive oil
- ½ teaspoon garlic powder

Directions:
1. Slice the cauliflower head into the steaks and rub with ground turmeric, cayenne pepper, and garlic powder.
2. Then line the baking tray with baking paper and put the cauliflower steaks inside.
3. Sprinkle them with olive oil and bake at 375f for 25 minutes or until the vegetable steaks are tender.

Nutrition Info:
- 92 calories,2.4g protein, 6.8g carbohydrates, 7.2g fat, 3.1g fiber, 0mg cholesterol, 34mg sodium, 366mg potassium.

Honey sweet potato bake

Servings:4
Cooking time: 20 minutes
Ingredients:
- 4 sweet potatoes, baked
- 1 tablespoon honey
- 1 teaspoon ground cinnamon
- ¼ teaspoon ground cardamom
- 1/3 cup soy milk

Directions:
1. Peel the sweet potatoes and mash them.
2. Then mix mashed potato with ground cinnamon, cardamom, and soy milk. Stir it well.
3. Transfer the mixture in the baking pan and flatten well.
4. Sprinkle the mixture with honey and cover with foil.
5. Bake the meal at 375f for 20 minutes.

Nutrition Info:
- 30 calories,0.7g protein, 6.5g carbohydrates, 0.4g fat, 0.5g fiber, 0mg cholesterol, 11mg sodium, 39mg potassium

Servings:6

Cooking time: 14 minutes

Ingredients:

- 1-pound tempeh, cubed
- ¼ cup low-sodium tamari
- 1 teaspoon nutritional yeast

Directions:

1. Mix up tamari and nutritional yeast.
2. Then dip the tempeh cubes in the liquid and transfer in the lined with a baking paper baking tray.
3. Bake the tempeh for 14 minutes at 385f. Flip the tempeh cubes on another side after 7 minutes of cooking.

Nutrition Info:

- 154 calories,14.8g protein, 8.3g carbohydrates, 8.2g fat, 0.2g fiber, 0mg cholesterol, 361mg sodium, 344mg potassium.

Quinoa burger

Servings:4

Cooking time: 20 minutes

Ingredients:

- 1/3 cup chickpeas, cooked
- ½ cup quinoa, cooked
- 1 teaspoon italian seasonings
- 1 teaspoon olive oil
- ½ onion, minced

Directions:

1. Blend the chickpeas until they are smooth.
2. Then mix them up with quinoa, italian seasonings, and minced onion. Stir the ingredients until homogenous.
3. After this, make the burgers from the mixture and place them in the lined baking tray.
4. Sprinkle the quinoa burgers with olive oil and bake them at 275f for 20 minutes.

Nutrition Info:

- 158 calories,6.4g protein, 25.2g carbohydrates, 3.8g fat, 4.7g fiber, 1mg cholesterol, 6mg sodium, 286mg potassium.

Servings:4

Cooking time: 10 minutes

Ingredients:

- 1 cup carrot, grated
- 1 tablespoon semolina
- 1 egg, beaten
- 1 teaspoon italian seasonings
- 1 tablespoon sesame oil

Directions:

1. In the mixing bowl, mix up grated carrot, semolina, egg, and italian seasonings.
2. Heat up sesame oil in the skillet.
3. Make the carrot cakes with the help of 2 spoons and put in the skillet.
4. Roast the cakes for 4 minutes per side.

Nutrition Info:

- 70 calories,1.9g protein, 4.8g carbohydrates, 4.9g fat, 0.8g fiber, 42mg cholesterol, 35mg sodium, 108mg potassium.

Loaded potato skins

Servings:6

Cooking time: 45 minutes

Ingredients:

- 6 potatoes
- 1 teaspoon ground black pepper
- 2 tablespoons olive oil
- ½ teaspoon minced garlic
- ¼ cup of soy milk

Directions:

1. Preheat the oven to 400f.
2. Pierce the potatoes with the help of the knife 2-3 times and bake in the oven for 30 minutes or until the vegetables are tender.
3. After this, cut the baked potatoes into the halves and scoop out the potato meat in the bowl.
4. Sprinkle the scooped potato halves with olive oil and ground black pepper and return back in the oven. Bake them for 15 minutes or until they are light brown.
5. Meanwhile, mash the scooped potato meat and mix it up with soy milk and minced garlic.
6. Fill the cooked potato halves with mashed potato mixture.

Nutrition Info:

- 194 calories, 4g protein, 34.4g carbohydrates, 5.1g fat, 5.3g fiber, 0mg cholesterol, 18mg sodium, 884mg potassium.

Servings:3
Cooking time: 30 minutes
Ingredients:

- 2 cups spinach, chopped
- 4 oz artichoke hearts, chopped
- ¼ cup low-fat yogurt
- 1 teaspoon italian seasonings
- 2 oz vegan mozzarella, shredded

Directions:

1. Mix up all ingredients in the casserole mold and cover it with foil.
2. Then transfer it in the preheated to 365f oven and bake it for 30 minutes.

Nutrition Info:

- 102 calories,3.7g protein, 11g carbohydrates, 4.9g fat, 2.5g fiber, 2mg cholesterol, 206mg sodium, 300mg potassium.

Tempeh reuben

Servings:4
Cooking time: 10 minutes
Ingredients:

- 10 oz tempeh
- ½ cup low-sodium vegetable broth
- 1 teaspoon apple cider vinegar
- 1 teaspoon garlic powder
- 1 tablespoon olive oil

Directions:

1. In the bowl mix up the vegetable broth, apple cider vinegar, and garlic powder.
2. Then put tempeh in the liquid and leave it to marinate for 15-20 minutes.
3. After this, cut tempeh into servings and put in the well-preheated skillet.
4. Add olive oil and cook it for 4 minutes per side or until golden brown.

Nutrition Info:

- 171 calories,13.5g protein, 7.3g carbohydrates, 11.2g fat, 0.1g fiber, 0mg cholesterol, 47mg sodium, 302mg potassium.

Servings:4

Cooking time: 25 minutes

Ingredients:

- 2 cups cauliflower florets
- 1 tablespoon ground turmeric
- 1 teaspoon smoked paprika
- 1 tablespoon olive oil

Directions:

1. Sprinkle the cauliflower florets with ground turmeric, smoked paprika, and olive oil.
2. Then line the baking tray with baking paper and put the cauliflower florets in the tray in one layer.
3. Bake the meal for 25 minutes at 375f or until the cauliflower florets are tender.

Nutrition Info:

- 50 calories,1.2g protein, 4.1g carbohydrates, 3.8g fat, 1.8g fiber, 0mg cholesterol, 16mg sodium, 207mg potassium.

Oregano pork tenderloin

Servings:4
Cooking time: 60 minutes
Ingredients:
- 1-pound pork tenderloin
- 1 tablespoon dried oregano
- 2 tablespoons avocado oil
- 1 teaspoon onion powder
- 1 teaspoon lime zest, grated

Directions:
1. Rub the pork tenderloin with dried oregano, onion powder, and lime zest.
2. Then brush it with avocado oil and wrap in the foil.
3. Bake the meat at 375f for 60 minutes.
4. Slice the cooked meat into servings.

Nutrition Info:
- 177 calories, 30g protein, 1.7g carbohydrates, 5g fat, 0.9g fiber, 83mg cholesterol, 68mg sodium, 525mg potassium.

Hoisin pork

Servings:4
Cooking time: 14 minutes
Ingredients:
- 1-pound pork loin steaks
- 2 tablespoons hoisin sauce
- 1 tablespoon apple cider vinegar
- 1 teaspoon olive oil

Directions:
1. Rub the pork steaks with hoisin sauce, apple cider vinegar, and olive oil.
2. Then preheat the grill to 395f.
3. Put the pork steak in the grill and cook them for 7 minutes per side.

Nutrition Info:
- 263 calories,39.3g protein, 3.6g carbohydrates, 10.1g fat, 0.2g fiber, 0mg cholesterol, 130mg sodium, 12mg potassium.

Servings:4

Cooking time: 30 minutes

Ingredients:

- 4 white cabbage leaves
- ½ cup carrot, grated
- 1 teaspoon italian seasonings
- ¼ cup tomato puree
- 6 oz lean ground pork

Directions:

1. In the mixing bowl, mix up italian seasonings, carrot, and lean ground pork.
2. Then fill the white cabbage leaves with meat mixture to get the cabbage rolls and put in the small casserole mold.
3. Add tomato puree and transfer in the preheated to 365f oven.
4. Cook the cabbage rolls for 30 minutes.

Nutrition Info:

- 80 calories,11.7g protein, 3.8g carbohydrates, 1.9g fat, 1g fiber, 32mg cholesterol, 41mg sodium, 318mg potassium.

Fennel pork chops

Servings:4

Cooking time: 35 minutes

Ingredients:

- 4 top pork loin chops
- 1 tablespoon fennel seeds
- 1 tablespoon margarine
- ½ cup water, hot

Directions:

1. Toss margarine in the skillet and add fennel seeds.
2. Roast the condiments for 2 minutes or until they start to smell.
3. After this, add pork chops and broil them on high heat for 4 minutes per side.
4. Add hot water and bring the meat to boil.
5. Transfer the skillet with pork chops in the preheated to 375f oven and cook it for 25 minutes.

Nutrition Info:

- 224 calories, 26.2g protein, 0.8g carbohydrates, 12g fat, 0.6g fiber, 65mg cholesterol, 84mg sodium, 451mg potassium.

Servings:3
Cooking time: 15 minutes

Ingredients:

- 9 oz beef tenders
- 2 tablespoons cayenne pepper
- 1 tablespoon lemon juice
- 2 tablespoons canola oil

Directions:

1. Cut the beef tenders into the strips and rub with cayenne pepper.
2. Sprinkle the meat with lemon juice and put it in the hot skillet.
3. Add canola oil and roast the meat for 15 minutes on medium heat. Stir it from time to time to avoid burning.

Nutrition Info:

- 231 calories, 22.5g protein, 2.1g carbohydrates, 14.6g fat, 1g fiber, 54mg cholesterol, 62mg sodium, 327mg potassium.

Spiced beef

Servings:4
Cooking time: 80 minutes

Ingredients:

- 1-pound beef sirloin
- 1 tablespoon five-spice seasoning
- 1 bay leaf
- 2 cups of water
- 1 teaspoon peppercorn

Directions:

1. Rub the meat with five-spice seasoning and put in the saucepan.
2. Add nay leaf, water, and peppercorns.
3. Close the lid and simmer it for 80 minutes on the medium heat.
4. Chop the cooked meat and sprinkle it with hot spiced water from the saucepan.

Nutrition Info:

- 213 calories,34.5g protein, 0.5g carbohydrates, 7.1g fat, 0.2g fiber, 101mg cholesterol, 116mg sodium, 466mg potassium.

Servings:4

Cooking time: 12 minutes

Ingredients:

- 4 pork loin chops, cubed
- 4 teaspoons spinach, blended

Directions:

1. Mix up pork chops and blended spinach.
2. Then preheat the grill to 400f.
3. Put the meat cubes in the grill and roast them for 6 minutes per side or until the meat is light brown.

Nutrition Info:

- 256 calories, 18g protein, 0g carbohydrates, 19.9g fat, 0g fiber, 69mg cholesterol, 57mg sodium, 279mg potassium.

Fajita pork strips

Servings:4

Cooking time: 35 minutes

Ingredients:

- 16 oz pork sirloin
- 1 tablespoon fajita seasonings
- 1 tablespoon canola oil

Directions:

1. Cut the pork sirloin into the strips and sprinkle with fajita seasonings and canola oil.
2. Then transfer the meat in the baking tray in one layer.
3. Bake it for 35 minutes at 365f. Stir the meat every 10 minutes during cooking.

Nutrition Info:

- 184 calories,18.5g protein, 1.3g carbohydrates, 10.8g fat, 0g fiber, 64mg cholesterol, 157mg sodium, 0mg potassium.

Servings:4
Cooking time: 14 minutes

Ingredients:

- 4 pork top loin chops
- 1 tablespoon herbs de provence
- 4 teaspoons olive oil

Directions:

1. Tub the pork chops with herbs de provence and sprinkle with olive oil.
2. After this, preheat the grill to 390f.
3. Put the pork chops in the grill and roast them for 7 minutes per side.

Nutrition Info:

- 231 calories,25.9g protein, 0g carbohydrates, 13.6g fat, 0g fiber, 65mg cholesterol, 48mg sodium, 425mg potassium.

Tender pork medallions

Servings:3
Cooking time: 25 minutes

Ingredients:

- 12 oz pork tenderloin
- 1 teaspoon dried sage
- 1 tablespoon margarine
- 1 teaspoon ground black pepper
- ½ cup low-fat yogurt

Directions:

1. Cut the pork tenderloin into 3 medallions and sprinkle with sage and ground black pepper.
2. Heat up margarine in the saucepan and add pork medallions.
3. Roast them for 5 minutes per side.
4. Then add yogurt and coat the meat in it well.
5. Close the lid and simmer the medallions for 15 minutes over the medium heat.

Nutrition Info:

- 227 calories,32.4g protein, 3.5g carbohydrates, 8.3g fat, 0.3g fiber, 85mg cholesterol, 138mg sodium, 586mg potassium.

Servings:3
Cooking time: 40 minutes
Ingredients:

- 12 oz beef tenderloin
- 1 teaspoon dried rosemary
- 1 onion, chopped
- 1 tablespoon avocado oil

Directions:

1. Cut the meat into the tenders and sprinkle with rosemary and avocado oil.
2. Then transfer it in the lined baking tray. Top the meat with onion and cover with foil.
3. Bake the meat for 30 minutes at 365f.
4. Then shake the meat well and cook it without foil for 10 minutes more.

Nutrition Info:

- 265 calories,33.3g protein, 3.9g carbohydrates, 11.1g fat, 1.2g fiber, 104mg cholesterol, 69mg sodium, 477mg potassium.

Chicken with red onion

Servings:4
Cooking time: 30 minutes

Ingredients:

- 1-pound chicken breasts, skinless, boneless, roughly cubed
- 3 red onions, sliced
- 2 tablespoons olive oil
- 1 cup of water
- 1 teaspoon dried thyme

Directions:

1. Heat up a pan with the oil over medium heat, add the onions and sauté for 10 minutes stirring often.
2. Add the chicken and cook for 3 minutes more.
3. Then add water, thyme, and stir the meal well.
4. Cook it for 15 minutes more.

Nutrition Info:

- 223 calories, 25g protein, 7.9g carbohydrates, 9.9g fat, 1.9g fiber, 73mg cholesterol, 63mg sodium, 543mg potassium.

Servings:4

Cooking time: 25 minutes

Ingredients:

- 1-pound chicken fillet, sliced
- 1 teaspoon ground clove
- 1 tablespoon avocado oil
- ½ cup tomato, chopped
- ¼ cup of water

Directions:

1. Heat up oil in the saucepan.
2. Add chicken and ground clove and stir the meal for 10 minutes.
3. After this, add tomato and water.
4. Close the lid and simmer the meal for 15 minutes more.

Nutrition Info:

- 226 calories,33.1g protein, 1.4g carbohydrates, 9g fat, 0.6g fiber, 101mg cholesterol, 100mg sodium, 346mg potassium.

Chicken tomato mix

Servings:4

Cooking time: 30 minutes

Ingredients:

- 1-pound chicken breast, skinless, boneless, chopped
- 1 cup tomatoes, chopped
- 1 chili pepper
- 1 tablespoon margarine
- ¼ cup of water

Directions:

1. Heat up margarine and add chili pepper. Roast it for 2 minutes.
2. Add chicken breast and stir the mixture well. Cook it for 8 minutes.
3. Then add tomatoes and water.
4. Close the lid and cook the meal for 20 minutes.

Nutrition Info:

- 163 calories,24.5g protein, 1.9g carbohydrates, 5.8g fat, 0.6g fiber, 73mg cholesterol, 94mg sodium, 530mg potassium.

Servings:4

Cooking time: 35 minutes

Ingredients:

- 1 cup green olives, pitted and halved
- 1 pound turkey fillet, sliced
- 1 tablespoon parsley, chopped
- 1 cup tomato puree
- 1 tablespoon olive oil

Directions:

1. Grease a baking dish with the oil.
2. Add all remaining ingredients in the baking pan, flatten well, and cover with foil.
3. Bake the meal ta 385f for 35 minutes.

Nutrition Info:

- 200 calories,24.9g protein, 7.8g carbohydrates, 7.8g fat, 2.3g fiber, 59mg cholesterol, 568mg sodium, 282mg potassium.

Soft sage turkey

Servings:4

Cooking time: 35 minutes

Ingredients:

- 1-pound turkey fillet, chopped
- 1 tablespoon margarine, melted
- 1 teaspoon dried sage
- 1 tablespoon olive oil

Directions:

1. Mix up olive oil, margarine, and sage in the shallow bowl.
2. Mix up turkey fillet and oil mixture together, and transfer in the baking pan.
3. Bake the meal at 375f for 35 minutes.

Nutrition Info:

- 163 calories,23.6g protein, 0.1g carbohydrates, 6.9g fat, 0.1g fiber, 59mg cholesterol, 290mg sodium, 3mg potassium.

Servings:4

Cooking time: 30 minutes

Ingredients:

- 1-pound chicken wings, skinless, boneless
- 1 tablespoon five-spices
- 2 tablespoons margarine, melted

Directions:

1. Rub the chicken wings with condiments and sprinkle with margarine.
2. Bake the chicken wings for 30 minutes at 365f.

Nutrition Info:

- 272 calories,32.9g protein, 1.6g carbohydrates, 14.1g fat, 0g fiber, 101mg cholesterol, 195mg sodium, 279mg potassium.

Thai style chicken cubes

Servings:6

Cooking time: 35 minutes

Ingredients:

- 16 oz chicken fillet, cubed
- 1 tablespoon scallions, chopped
- ½ cup thai chili sauce

Directions:

1. Heat up a pan over medium-high heat, add chicken and roast it for 5 minutes on each side, transfer to a baking dish, add chili sauce and scallions, toss well and transfer the meal in the preheated to 390f oven.
2. Bake the meal for 35 minutes.

Nutrition Info:

- 145 calories,21.9g protein, 0.3g carbohydrates, 5.6g fat, 0g fiber, 67mg cholesterol, 70mg sodium, 186mg potassium.

Servings:4

Cooking time: 25 minutes

Ingredients:

- 1 pound chicken breasts, skinless, boneless, chopped
- 2 cups of water
- 1 tablespoon sesame oil
- 1 cup butternut squash, chopped
- 1 teaspoon cayenne pepper

Directions:

1. Heat up a pan with the oil over medium-high heat, add the chicken and cook for 5 minutes.
2. Add all remaining ingredients and cook the meal for 20 minutes.

Nutrition Info:

- 263 calories, 33.2g protein, 4.3g carbohydrates, 11.9g fat, 0.8g fiber, 101mg cholesterol, 103mg sodium, 409mg potassium.

Asparagus chicken mix

Servings:4

Cooking time: 25 minutes

Ingredients:

- 1-pound chicken breast, skinless, boneless, chopped
- 2 tablespoons avocado oil
- 1 cup asparagus, trimmed and halved
- ½ teaspoon smoked paprika
- 2 cups tomatoes, chopped

Directions:

1. Heat up a pan with the oil over medium-high heat, add the chicken and asparagus, stir and cook for 5 minutes.
2. All remaining ingredients and cook the meal for 20 minutes over the medium-high heat.

Nutrition Info:

- 162 calories,25.7g protein, 5.3g carbohydrates, 4g fat, 2.2g fiber, 73mg cholesterol, 63mg sodium, 729mg potassium.

Servings:4

Cooking time: 40 minutes

Ingredients:

- 4 chicken thighs, skinless, boneless
- ½ teaspoon ground black pepper
- 1 cup apples, chopped
- ½ cup apple juice
- 1 teaspoon margarine

Directions:

1. Heat up margarine in the saucepan.
2. Add chicken and roast it for 5 minutes per side.
3. After this, add all remaining ingredients and close the lid.
4. Simmer the chicken for 30 minutes.

Nutrition Info:

- 330 calories,42.5g protein, 11.4g carbohydrates, 11.9g fat, 1.5g fiber, 130mg cholesterol, 139mg sodium, 449mg potassium.

Lean chicken thighs

Servings:4

Cooking time: 25 minutes

Ingredients:

- ½ teaspoon ground black pepper
- ½ teaspoon ground paprika
- ½ teaspoon garlic powder
- 1 tablespoon sesame oil
- 4 chicken thighs, boneless, skinless

Directions:

1. Rub the chicken thighs with ground black pepper, paprika, and garlic powder
2. The heat up the skillet and pour oil inside.
3. Add chicken thighs and cook them for 10 minutes. Flip the chicken on another side and cook for 10 minutes more.

Nutrition Info:

- 310 calories,42.4g protein, 0.6g carbohydrates, 14.3g fat, 0.2g fiber, 130mg cholesterol, 126mg sodium, 368mg potassium.

Servings:4

Cooking time: 25 minutes

Ingredients:

- 1 teaspoon ground paprika
- 1 teaspoon tomato paste
- 1 tablespoon olive oil
- 1-pound chicken fillet, chopped

Directions:

1. Mix up all ingredients in the baking pan and cover with foil.
2. Bake the chopped chicken for 30 minutes at 375f.

Nutrition Info:

- 248 calories, 33g protein, 0.6g carbohydrates, 12g fat, 0.3g fiber, 101mg cholesterol, 99mg sodium, 301mg potassium.

Oregano turkey tenders

Servings:4

Cooking time: 10 minutes

Ingredients:

- 2 turkey breast fillets, skinless, boneless
- 1 tablespoon dried oregano
- 1 tablespoon olive oil

Directions:

1. Cut the chicken fillets into the tenders and sprinkle with dried oregano and olive oil.
2. Then put the turkey tenders in the skillet in one layer and cook them for 5 minutes from each side or until the tenders are golden brown.

Nutrition Info:

- 101 calories,13.5g protein, 1.2g carbohydrates, 4.8g fat, 0.2g fiber, 30mg cholesterol, 240mg sodium, 6mg potassium.

Servings:8
Cooking time: 30 minutes
Ingredients:

- 8 chicken thighs, boneless and skinless
- ½ cup balsamic vinegar
- 3 tablespoon garlic, minced
- 1 teaspoon ground black pepper
- 3 tablespoons hot chili sauce

Directions:

1. Put the oil in a baking dish, add chicken, and remaining ingredients.
2. Toss well and bake at 425f for 30 minutes.

Nutrition Info:

- 286 calories, 42.5g protein, 1.4g carbohydrates, 10.9g fat, 0.2g fiber, 130mg cholesterol, 270mg sodium, 389mg potassium.

Spiced turkey fillet

Servings:4
Cooking time: 30 minutes
Ingredients:

- 2 tablespoons canola oil
- 1 red onion, chopped
- 2 tablespoons oregano
- 1-pound turkey fillet, chopped
- ½ cup of water

Directions:

1. Heat up canola oil in the saucepan.
2. Add turkey, oregano, and onion and cook the ingredients for 5 minutes.
3. Then add water and close the lid.
4. Simmer the meal for 25 minutes over medium heat.

Nutrition Info:

- 187 calories,24.1g protein, 4g carbohydrates, 7.8g fat, 1.6g fiber, 59mg cholesterol, 259mg sodium, 78mg potassium.

Dill steamed salmon

Servings:4
Cooking time: 0 minutes

Ingredients:

- 2 tablespoons dill, chopped
- 1 tablespoon low-fat cream cheese
- 1 teaspoon chili flakes
- 1 pound steamed salmon, chopped
- 1 red onion, diced

Directions:

1. Mix up all ingredients in the bowl and carefully stir until homogenous.

Nutrition Info:

- 174 calories,22.8g protein, 3.5g carbohydrates, 8g fat, 0.8g fiber, 53mg cholesterol, 62mg sodium, 531mg potassium

Grilled tilapia

Servings:4
Cooking time: 6 minutes

Ingredients:

- 1 tablespoon sesame oil
- ½ teaspoon ground black pepper
- ½ teaspoon garlic powder
- 4 medium tilapia fillets

Directions:

1. Sprinkle the fish with garlic powder, ground black pepper, and sesame oil.
2. Grill it for 3 minutes per side in the preheated to 400f grill.

Nutrition Info:

- 125 calories,21.1g protein, 0.4g carbohydrates, 4.4g fat, 0.1g fiber, 55mg cholesterol, 40mg sodium, 7mg potassium

Servings:4

Cooking time: 7 minutes

Ingredients:

- 1 tablespoon avocado oil
- 1 tablespoon lemon juice
- 1 tablespoon mint, chopped
- 1-pound cod fillet
- 2 tablespoons water

Directions:

1. Heat up a pan with the oil over medium heat, add mint and cod.
2. Cook the fish for 3 minutes per side.
3. Then add water and lemon juice. Cook the cod for 2 minutes more.

Nutrition Info:

- 97 calories,20.4g protein, 0.4g carbohydrates, 1.5g fat, 0.3g fiber, 56mg cholesterol, 72mg sodium, 22mg potassium

Clams stew

Servings:5

Cooking time: 10 minutes

Ingredients:

- 1-pound clams
- 1 teaspoon dried thyme
- 1 teaspoon ground paprika
- ½ cup light cream (low-fat)
- 1 tablespoon lemon juice

Directions:

1. Put dried thyme, ground paprika, and cream.
2. Bring the liquid to boil.
3. Then add lemon juice and whisk the mixture well.
4. Add clams and close the lid.
5. Simmer the clams stew for 5 minutes.

Nutrition Info:

- 94 calories,0.6g protein, 12g carbohydrates, 5.1g fat, 0.6g fiber, 16mg cholesterol, 345mg sodium, 96mg potassium

Servings:4

Cooking time: 6 minutes

Ingredients:

- 1-pound shrimps, peeled
- 1 lime
- 1 teaspoon lemon juice
- ½ teaspoon white pepper

Directions:

1. Cut the lime into wedges.
2. Then sprinkle the shrimps with lemon juice and white pepper.
3. String the lime and lime wedges in the wooden skewers one-by-one.
4. Preheat the grill to 400f.
5. Put the shrimp skewers in grill and cook for 3 minutes from each side or until the shrimps become light pink.

Nutrition Info:

- 141 calories, 26g protein, 3.7g carbohydrates, 2g fat, 0.6g fiber, 239mg cholesterol, 277mg sodium, 214mg potassium.

Juicy scallops

Servings:4

Cooking time: 5 minutes

Ingredients:

- 12 oz sea scallops
- 2 tablespoons olive oil
- ½ teaspoon garlic powder
- ¼ cup low-fat yogurt

Directions:

1. Sprinkle the scallops with garlic powder and olive oil and toss them in the hot skillet.
2. Roast the scallops for 3 minutes per side or until they are light brown.
3. Add yogurt and cook the seafood for 2 minutes more.

Nutrition Info:

- 147 calories,15.2g protein, 3.3g carbohydrates, 7.8g fat, 0g fiber, 29mg cholesterol, 148mg sodium, 314mg potassium

Servings:4

Cooking time: 0 minutes

Ingredients:

- 2 tablespoons canola oil
- ½ teaspoon lemon juice
- 1 cup corn kernels, cooked
- 1-pound salmon, canned, shredded
- 1 tablespoon scallions, chopped

Directions:

1. Put all ingredients in the bowl and mix up the salad.

Nutrition Info:

- 246 calories,23.3g protein, 7.4g carbohydrates, 14.5g fat, 1.1g fiber, 50mg cholesterol, 56mg sodium, 544mg potassium

Spicy ginger seabass

Servings:4

Cooking time: 10 minutes

Ingredients:

- 1 tablespoon ginger, grated
- 2 tablespoons sesame oil
- ¼ teaspoon chili powder
- 4 sea bass fillets, boneless
- 1 tablespoon margarine

Directions:

1. Heat up sesame oil and margarine in the skillet.
2. Add chili powder and ginger.
3. Then add seabass and cook the fish for 3 minutes per side.
4. Then close the lid and simmer the fish for 3 minutes over low heat.

Nutrition Info:

- 216 calories, 24g protein, 1.1g carbohydrates, 12.3g fat, 0.2g fiber, 54mg cholesterol, 123mg sodium, 354mg potassium

Servings:4

Cooking time: 10 minutes

Ingredients:

- 1-pound tuna fillet, chopped
- 1 tablespoon olive oil
- ½ cup shallot, chopped
- 2 tablespoons lime juice
- ½ cup of water

Directions:

1. Heat up a pan with the oil over medium-high heat, add shallots and sauté for 3 minutes.
2. Add the fish and cook it for 4 minutes on each side.
3. Then sprinkle the fish with lime juice and water.
4. Close the lid and simmer the tuna for 3 minutes.

Nutrition Info:

- 458 calories,24.3g protein, 3.9g carbohydrates, 38.7g fat, 0g fiber, 0mg cholesterol, 5mg sodium, 73mg potassium

Tomato halibut fillets

Servings:4

Cooking time: 10 minutes

Ingredients:

- 2 teaspoon sesame oil
- 4 halibut fillets, skinless
- 1 cup cherry tomatoes, halved
- 1 teaspoon dried basil

Directions:

1. Sprinkle the fish with basil and put in the hot skillet.
2. Add sesame oil and cherry tomatoes.
3. Roast the meal for 4 minutes and then stir well and cook for 5 minutes more.

Nutrition Info:

- 346 calories,60.9g protein, 1.8g carbohydrates, 9.1g fat, 0.5g fiber, 93mg cholesterol, 158mg sodium, 1414mg potassium

Servings:4

Cooking time: 14 minutes

Ingredients:

- 2 tablespoons avocado oil
- 4 salmon fillets, skinless
- 1 teaspoon dried basil
- ½ teaspoon garlic powder

Directions:

1. Heat up a pan with the olive oil, add the fish and cook for 4 minutes per side.
2. Sprinkle the cooked salmon with garlic powder and basil.

Nutrition Info:

- 246 calories,34.7g protein, 0.7g carbohydrates, 11.9g fat, 0.3g fiber, 78mg cholesterol, 79mg sodium, 710mg potassium

Salmon in capers

Servings:4

Cooking time: 15 minutes

Ingredients:

- 2 tablespoons avocado oil
- 1-pound salmon fillet, chopped
- 1 tablespoon capers, drained
- ½ cup low-fat milk

Directions:

1. Heat up a pan with the oil over medium-high heat, add salmon and roast it for 5 minutes.
2. Add capers and milk and saute the meal for 10 minutes over the medium heat.

Nutrition Info:

- 173 calories,23.2g protein, 2g carbohydrates, 8.2g fat, 0.4g fiber, 52mg cholesterol, 127mg sodium, 504mg potassium

Servings:5

Cooking time: 10 minutes

Ingredients:

- 1 pound shrimp, peeled
- 1 tablespoon margarine
- ¼ cup low-fat yogurt
- 1 teaspoon lemon zest, grated
- 1 chili pepper, chopped

Directions:

1. Melt the margarine in the skillet, add chili pepper, and roast it for 1 minute.
2. Then add shrimps and lemon zest.
3. Roast the shrimps for 2 minutes per side.
4. After this, add yogurt, stir the shrimps well and cook for 5 minutes.

Nutrition Info:

- 137 calories,21.4g protein, 2.4g carbohydrates, 4g fat, 0.1g fiber, 192mg cholesterol, 257mg sodium, 187mg potassium

Turmeric pate

Servings:6

Cooking time: 10 minutes

Ingredients:

- 1-pound tuna, canned
- 3 teaspoons lemon juice
- ¼ cup low-fat yogurt
- 1 teaspoon ground cinnamon
- ½ teaspoon ground turmeric

Directions:

1. Put all ingredients in the food processor.
2. Blend the pate until smooth and transfer in the bowl.

Nutrition Info:

- 149 calories,20.7g protein, 0.9g carbohydrates, 6.3g fat, 0.1g fiber, 24mg cholesterol, 46mg sodium, 283mg potassium

Servings:4

Cooking time: 8 minutes

Ingredients:

- 12 oz tuna fillet
- 8 oz pineapple, peeled
- 1 teaspoon olive oil
- ¼ teaspoon ground fennel

Directions:

1. Chop the tuna and pineapple on medium size cubes and sprinkle with olive oil and ground fennel.
2. Then string them in the skewers and place them in the preheated to 400f grill.
3. Cook the kebobs for 4 minutes per side.

Nutrition Info:

- 347 calories,18.2g protein, 7.5g carbohydrates, 27.6g fat, 0.8g fiber, 0mg cholesterol, 1mg sodium, 64mg potassium.

Rosemary salmon

Servings:4

Cooking time: 12 minutes

Ingredients:

- 1-pound salmon fillet
- 4 teaspoons olive oil
- 4 teaspoons lemon juice
- 1 tablespoon dried rosemary

Directions:

1. Cut the salmon fillet into 4 servings.
2. Then rub the fillets with olive oil, lemon juice, and dried rosemary.
3. Put the salmon on the tray and bake it for 12 minutes at 400f.

Nutrition Info:

- 194 calories,22.1g protein, 0.6g carbohydrates, 11.8g fat, 0.4g fiber, 50mg cholesterol, 51mg sodium, 450mg potassium.

Servings:3

Cooking time: 10 minutes

Ingredients:

- 10 oz sole fillet
- 2 tablespoons margarine
- 1 tablespoon dill weed
- 1 teaspoon garlic powder
- ½ teaspoon cumin seeds

Directions:

1. Toss the margarine in the skillet.
2. Add cumin seeds and dill weed.
3. Melt the mixture and simmer it for 30 seconds.
4. Then cut the sole fillet on 2 servings and sprinkle with garlic powder.
5. Put the fish fillets in the melted margarine mixture.
6. Cook the fish for 3 minutes per side.

Nutrition Info:

- 185 calories,23.3g protein, 1.5g carbohydrates, 9.2g fat, 0.3g fiber, 64mg cholesterol, 191mg sodium, 380mg potassium.

Aromatic salmon with fennel seeds

Servings:5

Cooking time: 10 minutes

Ingredients:

- 4 medium salmon fillets, skinless and boneless
- 1 tablespoon fennel seeds
- 2 tablespoons olive oil
- 1 tablespoon lemon juice
- 1 tablespoon water

Directions:

1. Heat up olive oil in the skillet.
2. Add fennel seeds and roast them for 1 minute.
3. Add salmon fillets and sprinkle with lemon juice.
4. Add water and roast the fish for 4 minutes per side over the medium heat.

Nutrition Info:

- 301 calories,4.8g protein, 0.8g carbohydrates, 18.2g fat, 0.6g fiber, 78mg cholesterol, 81mg sodium, 713mg potassium

Servings:4

Cooking time: 5 minutes

Ingredients:

- 1-pound scallops
- 1 teaspoon cajun seasonings
- 1 tablespoon olive oil

Directions:

1. Rub the scallops with cajun seasonings.
2. Heat up olive oil in the skillet.
3. Add scallops and cook them for 2 minutes per each side.

Nutrition Info:

- 130 calories, 19g protein, 2.7g carbohydrates, 4.4g fat, 0g fiber, 37mg cholesterol, 195mg sodium, 365mg potassium.

Allspice shrimps

Servings:4

Cooking time: 8 minutes

Ingredients:

- 1 teaspoon allspice, ground
- 2 tablespoons olive oil
- 1-pound shrimps, peeled

Directions:

1. Heat up olive oil in the skillet.
2. Mix up allspices and shrimps in the bowl.
3. Then transfer the seafood in the hot oil and cook for 3 minutes per side or until the shrimps are bright pink.

Nutrition Info:

- 196 calories,25.9g protein, 2.1g carbohydrates, 9g fat, 0.1g fiber, 239mg cholesterol, 277mg sodium, 197mg potassium

Melon salad

Servings:4
Cooking time: 0 minutes
Ingredients:
- 1 cup melon, chopped
- 2 bananas, chopped
- 1 tablespoon low-fat cream cheese

Directions:
1. Mix up all ingredients and transfer them to the serving plates.

Nutrition Info:
- 75 calories,1.2g protein, 16.7g carbohydrates,1.1g fat, 1.9g fiber, 3mg cholesterol, 14mg sodium, 318mg potassium.

Grilled peaches

Servings:4
Cooking time: 4 minutes
Ingredients:
- 8 peaches, pitted, halved
- 1 teaspoon canola oil
- ½ teaspoon ground cinnamon

Directions:
1. Preheat the grill to 395f.
2. Meanwhile, sprinkle the peaches with ground cinnamon and canola oil.
3. Put the fruits in the grill and roast them for 2 minutes per side or until the peaches are tender.

Nutrition Info:
- 129 calories,2.8g protein, 28.2g carbohydrates, 2g fat, 4.8g fiber, 0mg cholesterol, 0mg sodium, 571mg potassium.

Servings:12
Cooking time: 7 minutes
Ingredients:
- 1 cup low-fat milk
- ½ cup margarine
- ½ cup of cocoa powder
- 1 teaspoon vanilla extract

Directions:
1. Heat up a pan with the milk over medium heat, add the margarine, stir and cook everything for 7 minutes.
2. Take this off heat, add the cocoa powder and whisk well.
3. Pour the mixture into a lined square pan, flatten ell and refrigerate in the fridge for 120 minutes.

Nutrition Info:
- 85 calories, 1.4g protein, 3.1g carbohydrates, 8.2g fat, 1.1g fiber, 1mg cholesterol, 98mg sodium, 125mg potassium.

Rhubarb with aromatic mint

Servings:4
Cooking time: 10 minutes
Ingredients:
- ¼ cup low-fat milk
- 2 cups rhubarb, roughly chopped
- 1 tablespoon liquid honey
- 1 tablespoon mint, chopped

Directions:
1. Bring the milk to boil, add mint and rhubarb.
2. Cook the dessert for 10 minutes over the low heat.
3. Then cool the meal and add liquid honey. Stir it.

Nutrition Info:
- 36 calories,1.1g protein, 8g carbohydrates,0.3g fat, 1.2g fiber, 1mg cholesterol, 10mg sodium, 208mg potassium.

Servings:12
Cooking time: 5 minutes
Ingredients:

- 3 cups low-fat milk
- 2 tablespoons coconut flakes
- 3 tablespoons corn starch
- 3 tablespoons of liquid honey

Directions:

1. Bring the milk to boil and add coconut flakes and corn starch.
2. Simmer the mousse for 2 minutes.
3. Cool the dessert and mix it up with liquid honey.

Nutrition Info:

- 53 calories, 2.1g protein, 9.8g carbohydrates, 0.9g fat, 0.1g fiber, 3mg cholesterol, 27mg sodium, 97mg potassium.

Cardamom black rice pudding

Servings:4
Cooking time: 20 minutes
Ingredients:

- 5 cups of water
- ½ cup agave syrup
- 2 cups wild rice
- 1 teaspoon ground cardamom

Directions:

1. Mix up rice, water, and ground cinnamon.
2. Cook the rice for 20 minutes.
3. Add agave syrup and stir the pudding well.

Nutrition Info:

- 413 calories,1.8g protein, 93.4g carbohydrates,0.9g fat, 5.1g fiber, 0mg cholesterol, 43mg sodium, 375mg potassium.

Servings:3
Cooking time: 0 minutes
Ingredients:

- 3 figs, raw
- 3 teaspoons low-fat goat cheese
- 1 tablespoon liquid honey
- 3 walnuts

Directions:

1. Make the cross on the top of every fig and scoop a small amount of the fig meat from them.
2. Then fill the figs with low-fat goat cheese and walnuts.
3. Sprinkle the fruits with liquid honey.

Nutrition Info:

- 203 calories,6.6g protein, 19.2g carbohydrates, 11.9g fat, 2.9g fiber, 15mg cholesterol, 51mg sodium, 140mg potassium.

Lime cream

Servings:4
Cooking time: 15 minutes
Ingredients:

- 3 cups low-fat milk
- ½ cup lime juice
- 1 teaspoon lime zest, grated
- ½ cup agave syrup
- 2 tablespoons potato starch

Directions:

1. Heat up milk and add lime zest, agave syrup, and potato starch.
2. Simmer the liquid for 5 minutes more. Stir ti constantly.
3. Then cool the milk mixture, add lime juice, and stir well.

Nutrition Info:

- 230 calories,6.3g protein, 49.4g carbohydrates,1.9g fat, 0.2g fiber, 9mg cholesterol, 114mg sodium, 323 potassium.

Servings:8
Cooking time: 15 minutes
Ingredients:

- 1 pie crust
- ¼ cup lemon juice
- ½ cup low-fat milk
- 3 egg yolks
- 2 tablespoons potato starch

Directions:

1. Pour milk in the saucepan.
2. Add starch, egg yolks, and lemon juice.
3. Whisk the liquid until smooth.
4. Simmer it for 6 minutes. Stir it constantly.
5. Then leave the mixture for 10-15 minutes to cool.
6. Pour the lemon mixture over the pie crust and flatten it well.

Nutrition Info:

- 181 calories,2.8g protein, 21.9g carbohydrates, 9.3g fat, 0.5g fiber, 79mg cholesterol, 182mg sodium, 66mg potassium.

Nigella mix

Servings:8
Cooking time: 10 minutes
Ingredients:

- 4 cups mango, chopped
- 1 teaspoon nigella seeds
- 1 teaspoon vanilla extract
- ½ cup apple juice
- 1 teaspoon cinnamon powder

Directions:

1. Mix up all ingredients together and transfer them in the serving bowls.

Nutrition Info:

- 64 calories, 0.7 protein, 14.2g carbohydrates,1g fat, 1.4g fiber, 0mg cholesterol, 2mg sodium, 155mg potassium.

Servings:6
Cooking time: 35 minutes
Ingredients:

- 6 pears, peeled
- 3 cups orange juice
- 1 teaspoon cardamom
- 1 cinnamon stick
- 1 anise star

Directions:

1. In the saucepan mix up orange juice, cardamom, cinnamon stick, and anise star.
2. Bring the liquid to boil.
3. Add peeled pears and close the lid.
4. Cook the fruits for 25 minutes on the medium heat.

Nutrition Info:

- 178 calories,1.6g protein, 45g carbohydrates, 0.6g fat, 6.8g fiber, 0mg cholesterol, 4mg sodium, 494mg potassium.

Cantaloupe mix

Servings:4
Cooking time: 0 minutes
Ingredients:

- 2 cups cantaloupe, chopped
- 2 teaspoons vanilla extract
- 2 teaspoons orange juice

Directions:

1. Mix up all ingredients in the bowl and leave for 5 minutes.
2. Then transfer the dessert in the serving plates.

Nutrition Info:

- 34 calories,0.7g protein, 6.9g carbohydrates,0.2g fat, 0.7g fiber, 0mg cholesterol, 13mg sodium, 217mg potassium.

Servings:4
Cooking time: 24 minutes
Ingredients:
- 1 cup strawberries
- 1 tablespoon honey
- 4 eggs, beaten
- 1 tablespoon potato starch
- 2 cups low-fat milk

Directions:
1. In a bowl, combine the strawberries with the honey and all remaining ingredients.
2. Pour the mixture in the ramekins and transfer in the oven.
3. Bake the pudding for 24 minutes at 375f.

Nutrition Info:
- 152 calories,9.9g protein, 16g carbohydrates, 5.7g fat, 0.7g fiber, 170mg cholesterol, 116mg sodium, 300mg potassium.

Baked apples

Servings:3
Cooking time: 35 minutes
Ingredients:
- 3 apples
- 3 pecans, chopped
- 1 tablespoon raisins, chopped
- 3 teaspoons liquid honey
- ½ teaspoon ground cardamom

Directions:
1. Scoop the tops of the apples to get the medium size holes.
2. Then fill the holes with pecans, raisins, and ground cardamom.
3. Add liquid honey and wrap the apples in the foil (separately – wrap each apple).
4. Bake the apples in the preheated to 380f oven for 35 minutes.

Nutrition Info:
- 245 calories,2.3g protein, 41.2g carbohydrates, 10.4g fat, 7.1g fiber, 0mg cholesterol, 3mg sodium, 327mg potassium.

Servings:4

Cooking time: 10 minutes

Ingredients:

- 4 apples, halved
- 2 tablespoons chia seeds
- 1 teaspoon vanilla extract
- 1 teaspoon ground cinnamon

Directions:

1. Rub the apples with vanilla extract and ground cinnamon and transfer in the preheated to 375f oven.
2. Bake the apple halves for 10 minutes.
3. Then sprinkle the apples with chia seeds.

Nutrition Info:

- 155 calories,1.8g protein, 34.4g carbohydrates,2.6g fat, 8.2g fiber, 0mg cholesterol, 3mg sodium, 271mg potassium.

Chia and pineapple bowl

Servings:4

Cooking time: 0 minutes

Ingredients:

- 3 cups pineapple, peeled and cubed
- 1 teaspoon chia seeds
- 1 teaspoon fresh mint, chopped\
- 1 tablespoon liquid honey

Directions:

1. Mix up all ingredients in the big bowl.
2. Then transfer the dessert in the serving bowls.

Nutrition Info:

- 89 calories,1.1g protein, 21.6g carbohydrates,0.9g fat, 2.6g fiber, 0mg cholesterol, 2mg sodium, 150mg potassium.

Servings:3

Cooking time: 0 minutes

Ingredients:

- 1 cup strawberries
- 1 cup melon, cubed
- 1 cup grapes
- 2 kiwis, cubed
- 1 cup watermelon, cubed

Directions:

1. String the fruits in the wooden skewers one-by-one.
2. Store the cooked fruit kebabs in the fridge, not more than 30 minutes.

Nutrition Info:

- 100 calories,1.8g protein, 24.4g carbohydrates, 0.7g fat, 3.4g fiber, 0mg cholesterol, 12mg sodium, 485mg potassium.

Citrus pudding

Servings:4

Cooking time: 15 minutes

Ingredients:

- 2 cups orange juice
- 2 tablespoons cornstarch
- ¼ cup of rice
- ¼ cup agave syrup

Directions:

1. Mix up orange juice and rice in the saucepan and bring it to boil. Simmer the mixture for 10 minutes.
2. Add rice and agave syrup and simmer the pudding for 5 minutes more.

Nutrition Info:

- 176 calories,1.6g protein, 42.4g carbohydrates,0.3g fat, 0.4g fiber, 0mg cholesterol, 16mg sodium, 274mg potassium.

Servings:6

Cooking time: 10 minutes

Ingredients:

- 16 ounces raspberries
- 2 tablespoons water
- 2 tablespoons lime juice
- ¼ teaspoon lime zest, grated
- 2 tablespoons cornstarch

Directions:

1. Put all ingredients except cornstarch in the saucepan and bring to boil.
2. Add cornstarch stir until it is smooth and cook for 2 minutes more.

Nutrition Info:

- 51 calories, 0.9g protein, 11.8g carbohydrates,0.5g fat, 5g fiber, 0mg cholesterol, 2mg sodium, 118mg potassium.

Vanilla cream

Servings:4

Cooking time: 10 minutes

Ingredients:

- 1 cup low-fat milk
- 1 cup fat-free cream cheese
- 1 teaspoon vanilla extract
- 2 tablespoons corn starch
- 4 teaspoons liquid honey

Directions:

1. Heat up a pan with the milk over medium heat, add the rest of the ingredients, whisk, and cook for 10 minutes on low heat.
2. Divide the mix into bowls and refrigerate the cream for 120 minutes in the fridge.

Nutrition Info:

- 123 calories,10.4g protein, 16.8g carbohydrates,1.4g fat, 0g fiber, 8mg cholesterol, 343mg sodium, 191mg potassium.

Servings:5
Cooking time: 0 minutes
Ingredients:

- 3 cups non-fat milk
- 1 teaspoon ginger, ground
- 2 teaspoons vanilla extract
- 1 cup nuts, chopped

Directions:

1. Blend the nuts until smooth and mix them up with ginger, milk, and vanilla extract. Stir well.

Nutrition Info:

- 223 calories,9.6g protein, 14.6g carbohydrates,14.1g fat, 2.5g fiber, 3mg cholesterol, 262mg sodium, 399mg potassium.

Mango rice

Servings:4
Cooking time: 30 minutes
Ingredients:

- ½ cup of rice
- 2 cups low-fat milk
- 1 mango, peeled and chopped
- 1 teaspoon vanilla extract
- ½ teaspoon ground cinnamon

Directions:

1. Bring the milk to a boil and add rice.
2. Simmer it for 25 minutes.
3. Add vanilla, cinnamon, and mango, stir and cool to the room temperature.

Nutrition Info:

- 190 calories,6.5g protein, 37.5g carbohydrates,1.7g fat, 1.8g fiber, 6mg cholesterol, 56mg sodium, 354mg potassium.

Servings:4

Cooking time: 0 minutes

Ingredients:

- 4 tablespoons cream cheese
- 1 cup apricot, chopped
- 1 teaspoon vanilla extract

Directions:

1. Blend all ingredients together until you get the creamy texture.
2. Transfer the dessert in the bowls.

Nutrition Info:

- 53 calories,1.1g protein, 3.9g carbohydrates,3.6g fat, 0.6g fiber, 11mg cholesterol, 30mg sodium, 85mg potassium.

Peach stew

Servings:4

Cooking time: 15 minutes

Ingredients:

- 2 cups peaches, halved
- 2 cups of water
- 1 tablespoon honey
- 2 tablespoons lemon juice

Directions:

1. Mix up all ingredients in the saucepan and simmer for 15 minutes over the low heat.

Nutrition Info:

- 47 calories,0.8g protein, 11.5g carbohydrates,0.3g fat, 1.2g fiber, 0mg cholesterol, 5mg sodium, 156mg potassium.

Servings:4

Cooking time: 15 minutes

Ingredients:

- 1 cup oatmeal, grinded
- 1 teaspoon vanilla extract
- 1 teaspoon honey
- 3 bananas, mashed

Directions:

1. Mix up mashed bananas and oatmeal.
2. Add vanilla extract and honey. Stir the mixture well.
3. Then line the baking tray with baking paper.
4. Make the small cookies from the banana mixture with the help of the spoon and put them in the prepared baking tray.
5. Bake the cookies for 15 minutes at 360f or until the cookies are light brown.

Nutrition Info:

- 165 calories,3.7g protein, 35.6g carbohydrates, 1.6g fat, 4.4g fiber, 0mg cholesterol, 2mg sodium, 393mg potassium.

Day 1

Breakfast:Chives And Sesame Omelets

Lunch:Oregano Pork Tenderloin

Dinner:Vegan Salad

Day 2

Breakfast:Omelet With Peppers

Lunch:Hoisin Pork

Dinner:Tender Green Beans Salad

Day 3

Breakfast:Cheese Hash Browns

Lunch:White Cabbage Rolls

Dinner:Fish Salad

Day 4

Breakfast:Egg Toasts

Lunch:Fennel Pork Chops

Dinner:Salad Skewers

Day 5

Breakfast:Curry Tofu Scramble

Lunch:Hot Beef Strips

Dinner:Fennel Bulb Salad

Day 6

Breakfast:Walnut Pudding

Lunch:Spiced Beef

Dinner:Watercress Salad

Breakfast: Fruits And Rice Pudding

Lunch:Spinach Pork Cubes

Dinner:Orange Mango Salad

Day 8

Breakfast:Vanilla Toasts

Lunch:Fajita Pork Strips

Dinner:Pine Nuts Salad

Day 9

Breakfast:Blueberries Mix

Lunch:Herbs De Provence Pork Chops

Dinner:Shredded Beef Salad

Day 10

Breakfast:Sweet Yogurt With Figs

Lunch:Tender Pork Medallions

Dinner:Seafood Salad With Grapes

Day 11

Breakfast:Strawberry Sandwich

Lunch:Baked Beef Tenders

Dinner:Tender Endives Salad

Day 12

Breakfast:Almond Crepes

Lunch:Chicken With Red Onion

Dinner:Smoked Salad

Day 13

Breakfast:Bean Frittata

Lunch:Clove Chicken

Dinner:Corn Salad With Spinach

Breakfast:Bean Casserole

Lunch:Chicken Tomato Mix

Dinner:Spring Salad

Day 15

Breakfast:Grape Yogurt

Lunch:Turkey With Olives

Dinner:Tropical Salad

Day 16

Breakfast:Cherry Rice

Lunch:Soft Sage Turkey

Dinner:Bean Sprouts Salad

Day 17

Breakfast:Whole Grain Pancakes

Lunch:5-spices Chicken Wings

Dinner:Tuna Salad

Day 18

Breakfast:Breakfast Almond Smoothie

Lunch:Thai Style Chicken Cubes

Dinner:Garlic Edamame Salad

Day 19

Breakfast:Baked Fruits

Lunch:Pumpkin Chicken

Dinner:Balsamic Vinegar Salad

Day 20

Breakfast:Chia Oatmeal

Lunch:Asparagus Chicken Mix

Dinner:Cucumber And Lettuce Salad

Breakfast:Millet Cream

Lunch:Apple Chicken

Dinner:Cauliflower Steaks